The
Happiest Kids
in the World

The Happiest Kids in the World

How Dutch Parents Help Their Kids (and Themselves) by Doing Less

RINA MAE ACOSTA
and MICHELE HUTCHISON

THE EXPERIMENT

NEW YORK

The Experiment, LLC, 220 East 23rd Street, Suite 301, New York, NY 10010-4674
theexperimentpublishing.com

This book contains the opinions and ideas of its author. The author and publisher are not engaged in rendering medical, health, or any other kind of personal professional services in the book. The author and publisher specifically disclaim all responsibility for any liability, loss, or risk—personal or otherwise—that is incurred directly or indirectly by the use and application of any of the contents of this book.

This book is a work of nonfiction based on the experiences and recollections of the authors and interviews with other parents and researchers. In some cases, names of people and identifying details have been changed to protect the identity of others. The authors have stated to the publishers that, except in some minor respects, the contents of this book are true.

Where the publisher was aware of a trademark claim, the designations have been capitalized.

The Experiment's books are available at special discounts when purchased in bulk for premiums and sales promotions as well as for fund-raising or educational use. For details, contact us at info@theexperimentpublishing.com.

Library of Congress Cataloging-in-Publication Data

Names: Acosta, Rina Mae, author. | Hutchison, Michele, author.
Title: The happiest kids in the world : how Dutch parents help their kids
   (and themselves) by doing less / Rina Mae Acosta, Michele Hutchison.
Description: New York : Experiment, [2017] | Includes bibliographical
   references and index.
Identifiers: LCCN 2016054448| ISBN 9781615193905 (pbk.) | ISBN 9781615193912
   (ebook)
Subjects: LCSH: Child rearing--Netherlands. | Parent and child--Netherlands.
Classification: LCC HQ792.N4 A26 2017 | DDC 649/.109492--dc23
LC record available at https://lccn.loc.gov/2016054448

ISBN 978-1-61519-390-5
Ebook ISBN 978-1-61519-391-2

Cover and text design by Sarah Smith
Cover background based on image © Alexandra Soloviova | Shutterstock
Cover illustration by Alyana Cazalet
Author photograph by Elma Coetzee

Manufactured in the United States of America
Distributed by Workman Publishing Company, Inc.
Distributed simultaneously in Canada by Thomas Allen & Son Ltd.

First printing April 2017
10 9 8 7 6 5 4 3 2 1

For our kids

Rina's Family

Rina Mae

I'm an Asian American writer who lives in a Dutch village with my husband, Bram, and our two boys. Originally from the San Francisco Bay Area, I love being an expat in Europe.

Bram

My husband, a Dutch entrepreneur who loves spending time with Julius and Matteo on his *Papadag*.

Bram Julius

Our first-born son, a lively child who loves discovering new things, bedtime stories and *hagelslag*.

Matteo

Our contented second baby, who wasn't the best sleeper at first but now loves a routine of eating, sleeping and playing.

Michele's Family

Michele

Originally from the Midlands (central England), I moved to Amsterdam when I was pregnant with my first baby. When I'm not translating or writing, I'm mainly gardening.

Martijn

My husband, a Dutch publisher and, ironically, a great Anglophile, who loves spending hours in the kitchen.

Ben

Our eldest child, who has recently started high school and is fanatic about dance.

Ina

Our daughter, an energetic, sporty girl with a passion for math.

"The best way to make children good is to make them happy"

—OSCAR WILDE

Contents

Introduction

Two toddlers have just chased each other to the top of a jungle gym and are jostling to get down the slide first. Their mothers are lost in conversation on a nearby park bench, sipping their lattes and feeling the weak sun on their faces. In the distance, a dog barks and a little boy ambles along on his balance bike, trailed by his grandfather who is pushing a stroller. A gang of older children in tracksuits comes racing along the bike path, laughing and joking, hockey sticks dangling dangerously close to their wheels. They overtake a young mom, who is cycling more slowly, balancing a baby in a seat on the front of her bike and a toddler on the back. A group of girls is playing monkey-in-the-middle on the grass, their joyful shrieks filling the air. Not far away, some boys are perfecting their skateboarding moves. None of the school-age children are accompanied by adults.

This happy scene isn't from a movie. It's just a regular Wednesday afternoon in springtime in Amsterdam's Vondelpark, a scene that's enacted all across the Netherlands every day.

In 2013, a UNICEF report rated Dutch children the happiest in the world.[1] According to researchers, Dutch kids are ahead of their peers in childhood well-being when compared with twenty-nine of the world's richest industrialized countries. The US ranked twenty-sixth, just above Lithuania, Latvia and Romania – the three poorest countries in the survey. Children from the Netherlands were in the top five in each of the categories assessed: Material Well-being; Health and Safety; Education; Behaviors and Risks; and Housing and Environment. In fact, the Dutch scored highest for Behaviors and Risks, as well as for Education (a category in which the US came in twenty-seventh). When it came to Dutch children rating their own happiness levels, more than 95 percent of them considered themselves happy. Several other research surveys have likewise highlighted the positive benefits of growing up in Holland – the OECD Better Life Index and the World Health Organization, for example. (The OECD is an organization promoting economic and social well-being around the world.) The UNICEF report was a follow-up to one conducted in 2007, in which the Netherlands was first heralded as a prime example of childhood prosperity. The US and the UK ranked in the two lowest positions.

In addition, new research also suggests that Dutch babies are happier than their American counterparts. After examining the temperamental differences between babies born in the US and in the Netherlands, Dutch babies were found to be more contented – laughing, smiling and cuddling more – than American babies. Dutch babies were also easier to soothe, while American babies displayed more fear, sadness and frustration. Psychologists attribute this discrepancy to the different cultural mores of child-rearing in the two countries.[2] It's quite astonishing to us that no one seems to be making more of a fuss about this.

As an American mom and a British mom, both of us married to Dutchmen and raising our kids in the Netherlands, we've found it hard not to notice how happy Dutch children are. The scene we described above should give you an idea why: Dutch children enjoy freedoms denied to children in the countries we come from, and thrive on them. Here are some of the things that set Dutch children apart from children in the US and the UK:

- Dutch babies get more sleep
- Dutch kids have little or no homework in elementary school
- Dutch kids are not just seen but also heard
- Dutch kids are trusted to ride their bikes to school on their own
- Dutch kids are allowed to play outside unsupervised
- Dutch kids have regular family meals

- Dutch kids get to spend more time with their moms and dads
- Dutch kids enjoy simple pleasures and are happy with secondhand toys

And, last but not least, Dutch kids get to eat chocolate sprinkles (*hagelslag*) for breakfast!

Childhood over here consists of lots of freedom, plenty of play and little academic stress. As a consequence, Dutch kids are pleasant to be around. Once you get past their blunt communication style, they are sociable, friendly, chatty, refreshingly honest and straight to the point. Dutch children are helpful and quick to take the initiative, and they don't demand the constant attention of grown-ups. They know how to entertain themselves.

When we say that we've noticed that children here are happy, we don't mean they are constantly leaping for joy, bouncing off the walls and spontaneously bursting into Pharrell Williams' "Happy." Dutch children are self-aware and confident, and are able to foster meaningful ties with family members, build loyal friendships, find love and discover their place in the world. This is the kind of happiness children experience when their parents listen to and respect their opinions.

Such an upbringing produces the most confident, responsible and respectful teenagers you may ever come across. Dutch teenagers don't rebel. They don't possess that posturing arrogance, but rather a mature self-assurance. Even though it is culturally acceptable to have romantic sleepovers, the Netherlands also boasts one of the lowest rates of teenage pregnancy in the world. These well-adjusted children grow up prepared to deal with the trials and tribulations of adult life.

The assertion made by the seventeenth-century philosopher John Locke that a child is born a blank slate who will be shaped by her environment permeates the standard American approach to child-rearing. Some say that this has led to a new normal of hyper-aware, highly opinionated and overly engaged parents. Their children – pressured to perform, pushed to conform, wired for success – are not allowed to develop at their own pace. English and American parents these days are much more engaged with their children than were parents of previous generations, and are inclined to believe that everything a child does requires vigilant adult supervision. The defining feature of modern-day parents in the US and the UK is anxiety: Our friends back home are running themselves ragged; every parenting decision is freighted with doubt, second thoughts and guilt. Why aren't Dutch parents weighed down by this anxiety? Why is it that they don't show the overanxious, helicoptering behavior so common elsewhere?

The Netherlands has a reputation for being a liberal country with a tolerance for sex, drugs and alcohol, yet beneath this lies a closely guarded secret: The Dutch are actually fairly conservative people. At the heart of Dutch culture is a society of home-loving people who place the child firmly at the center. Parents have a healthy attitude toward their kids, seeing them as individuals rather than as extensions of themselves. They understand that achievement doesn't necessarily lead to happiness, but that happiness can cultivate achievement. The Dutch have reined in the anxiety, stress and expectations of modern-day parenting, redefining the meaning of success and well-being. For them, success starts with happiness – that of their children and themselves.

The Dutch parenting style hits that elusive balance between parental involvement and benign neglect. It is authoritative, not authoritarian. The Dutch believe in good old-fashioned family values, coupled with a modern appreciation of a child's intrinsic worth and a respect for women's lives outside of motherhood. The norm in the Netherlands is simplicity: Families tend to choose simple, low-cost activities and take a down-to-earth approach. There is also an acceptance of different types of families. The Dutch family policy considers a family to be "every household of one or more adults who are responsible for the care and upbringing of one or more children."[3]

Dutch society has fought for and achieved an enviable work-life balance. As the part-time-work champions of Europe, the Dutch work on average twenty-nine hours a week, dedicate at least one day a week to spending time with their children, and pencil in time for themselves, too.[4] You won't find a Dutch mother expressing guilt about the amount of time she spends with her children – she will make a point of finding time for herself outside of motherhood and work. Sturdy, windswept and self-assured, these moms don't start to stress about getting back into shape the minute they leave the hospital with their new baby. And Dutch moms don't do for their children things they are capable of doing themselves – they believe in encouraging independence at the appropriate age. They are confident and calm. There's none of that "mompetition" or mommy guilt you see in the US and the UK.

Dutch fathers, especially those who are dads to babies and toddlers, believe in taking a more equal role in child-rearing and household chores. They look after their kids on their days off and help put the little ones to bed. You're just as likely to see a dad pushing a stroller or wearing a baby-carrier as a mom. And when a child has a temperature, for example, Dutch parents will take turns staying at home with the child, with most employers showing understanding and leniency. Dutch dads walk tall, talk straight and don't care if we expats make fun of their crispy gelled curls, red pants or yellow winter coats.

In contrast, we see American and British parents feeling constantly challenged and unsettled by their own unrealistic expectations, and by other people's opinions. There's an assumption that children need all the time, money, resources and attention a parent can (superhumanly) provide in order to give them a head start in life. This assumption seems to have become ingrained within US and UK culture. If moms don't live up to the ideal of the self-sacrificing, Pinterest-savvy, bending-over-backwards mommy, society is quick to wave a finger. But since when did being a good parent mean making child-rearing a life-defining pursuit? When did we come to accept that modern parenthood should be all work and no fun?

At the very crux of the judgmental bandwagon is the way society measures and compares parenting expertise through the academic accomplishments of our children. We are familiar with the middle-class parenting clichés of our own countries: ergonomic baby carriers, fancy strollers, organic snacks, exclusive private schools, sports clubs, music lessons. . . . The school playground has been transformed into a parenting battleground. A friend in New York described the back-stabbing melee to secure a nursery-school place on the Upper East Side. Parents and three-year-olds have to go through a rigorous selection process, and being rejected is worse than being left at the altar. There's even such a thing as "good" or "bad" birthdays, with conception timed to ensure that the child will be the eldest (and, the argument goes, therefore the most intellectually advanced) in the class. Competitive motherhood reaches its extreme in New York and London; from there, it permeates to other cities, to suburbs and villages. Parenting has evolved into a highly cutthroat, exhausting business and schooling into a war zone.

Here, however, in this small, flat Western European country, parents are doing things differently. And, as a result, they are raising some of the most contented children in the world. The German poet Heinrich Heine once joked, "When the world comes to an end, I shall go to Holland, for everything there happens fifty years later." There's something both familiar and old-fashioned about life in the Netherlands. Dutch children enjoy a huge degree of freedom: They ride their bikes to school, play on the streets and visit friends after school, all unaccompanied. Everyone has something to contribute to the conversation at the family dinner table, and families have time to do things together. Children in elementary school aren't expected to do homework, and they don't cram for exams. It's the kind of childhood that many of us are nostalgic for, or would have loved to have had. A childhood from black-and-white photographs, old movies and the pages of Judy Blume and Beverly Cleary books. The simple pleasures of childhood that Norman Rockwell so famously illustrated.

But is this version of childhood really so old-fashioned? Or is it perhaps ahead of its time? Might the Dutch have consciously clung to this vision of childhood? And what is it about the Netherlands that has allowed its children to still experience such a carefree existence? Is this small country really so much safer than other countries?[5]

The Netherlands is a wealthy Western European country that enjoys all the conveniences of modern life and suffers the attendant first world problems, including crime, murder and child abduction. However, there is no tabloid press whipping up parental anxiety, and Dutch parents are extremely good at putting things into perspective: They appraise the level of real risk to their child and act accordingly. The Dutch even have a word for this: *relativeren*. It means weighing up the pros and cons and, rather than worrying about child-snatchers, pedophiles or major disasters, preparing children for more common risks, like drowning or traffic accidents, by ensuring that they can swim, ride a bike and cross the road safely.

Crucially, although average Dutch household debt is among the highest in Europe, and the country isn't without its social problems, there is less social and financial inequality in the Netherlands than in the US and the UK. Living conditions are good, though not perfect for everyone. In the 2013 UNICEF report, the Netherlands trailed behind Switzerland, Ireland and Norway in the category Housing and Environment. Let's not forget, the country is quite damp (a large portion of the land lies below sea level), and seriously overpopulated. The perpetual grey skies can be downright depressing at times. It's no utopia.

As expat moms raising our children in the Netherlands, we'll give you the lowdown on the Dutch approach to parenting. We met a few months before embarking on the book, and though our backgrounds are very different and we live in different parts of the country, we have become the best of friends. Michele, whose children are older than Rina's, will focus on children of elementary-school age and up, and Rina on children under the age of five. Both of us have talked to parents and their children in an attempt to work out what it is that the Dutch know and their American and British counterparts have forgotten or overlooked. How do Dutch parents produce such happy kids, such pleasant teenagers? Could the answer really lie in the chocolate sprinkles they have on bread for breakfast? Is it the fact that Dutch children cycle everywhere? Is it the relaxed approach to parenting? The preference for home births? The Dutch love of dairy produce? The frequent camping holidays? The multitrack high school system? We've talked to other parents, and we've listened, and we'll share with you those aha! moments we've had along the way. And, we'll do what we can to give as many tips as possible to help you to raise your children the Dutch way: happy.

1

Discovering Dutchland

Rina in Doorn, a quaint Dutch village in the woods

My investigation into why Dutch children are so happy begins at my home in Doorn, a Dutch village with a population of ten thousand situated in the middle of a national park and populated by young families, pensioners, nature lovers and those seeking a slower pace of life. It's a place where you'll see children playing on tree-lined streets, where making delicious homemade pancakes and warm chocolate milk is considered a virtue, where families eat freshly made caramel waffles at the farmers' market, where the air is filled with the smell of barbecue smoke in the spring and summer, and of burning logs in the fall and winter, and where the best chance of making new friends, young and old, is on a walk in the local woods. It's also 5,478 miles from San Francisco – a place I called home for most of my life.

While I am connected to the filtered realities of life back in the Bay Area, thanks to my Facebook feed, Instagram notifications and Skype video dates, I'm living in a parallel universe. My parents worked their fingers to the bone on a laundry list of sacrifices; the mantra "we sacrificed everything for you to have a better life and a good education" played on repeat. They set the standards for academic excellence exceedingly high, and any failure or shortcoming brought family shame and loss of face. Ensuring that my brothers and I had a happy childhood was more of an afterthought, a footnote to more pressing concerns, as my parents struggled paycheck to paycheck to send us to the local private Catholic school, pay the mortgage, put food on the table, give money to relatives left behind in the Philippines, and keep up with the Santoses.

Childhood, it seemed, was something to be endured rather than enjoyed. Now, ironically, I am an American expat in a small Dutch village, navigating parenthood and exploring a new way to live, just like my parents, in a culture very different from my own.

It's all because of a love-at-first-sight, transatlantic romance that started when a Dutch graduate student was, literally, dropped off at my front doorstep. My cousin Grace, who had befriended the Dutch coed at the University of Florida, was convinced we were meant for each other. Since I was too preoccupied pursuing a career in medical research to care, she took matters into her own hands: She brought Bram to visit me in Philadelphia, pretending it was just an off-the-cuff visit. It happened to be Bram's last week in the United States before he headed back to Holland to finish his master's thesis.

No one expects to fall in love at first sight. I certainly didn't expect to open my door to a charming European who would profess to be madly in love with me just hours after our first hello. Luckily, I had enough common sense to at least give this Dutch boy a chance – from a distance of 3,721 miles across the Atlantic Ocean, of course. We had a good old-fashioned romance with a modern twist, him sending long, handwritten love letters as well as frequent emails, regular Gmail chats and spontaneous phone calls. And, for the first time in my life, I was honest with myself: I had to ask where my heart really lay – and it wasn't in becoming a doctor.

He proposed in Paris and we married in San Francisco. And here I am in Holland, ten years later, living in a rented 1930s cottage in the woods, contemplating the differences between the culture of the Netherlands and the US, and searching for a middle ground. Although I am very happy in my marriage, it took me a while to grow fond of life in the Low Countries. In fact, I struggled with it for the first seven years: The culture shock was immense, all-encompassing and unrelenting. The weather is persistently dark, rainy and cloudy, and I suffered from Seasonal Affective Disorder eleven months of the year. And there were other aspects of Dutch life I didn't like – for example, I found it difficult to accept how small everything seemed, and the way that everyone gave me advice I hadn't asked for.

When I became pregnant with my first child, Bram Julius, I was apprehensive. I suppose "anxious" is a more accurate description, really. I wanted my son to have what I hadn't had: a happy childhood. So I bought into the perfect-mom myth, an idealized (and unrealistic) vision of motherhood that demanded I dedicate myself to my child and devote unprecedented amounts of patience and understanding to him. I devoured all the (unsolicited) advice on what to do and what not to do in pregnancy, and various contradictory parenting philosophies. I signed up for prenatal and yoga classes and meticulously studied all the developmental milestones in the first year of a child's life. Well-meaning American friends and family showered me with flashcards, baby-sign-language tutorials, baby-led weaning manuals, Dr. Seuss books and *Sesame Street* DVDs.

I also started debating the pros and cons of the Montessori, Dalton, Regina Coeli and Waldorf methods of nursery schooling. After all, I reasoned, my baby will only have so much time to prepare his answers

Doe maar gewoon ...

There is a national saying that defines every facet of life in the Netherlands: *Doe maar gewoon dan doe je al gek genoeg* or, in its shortened form, *Doe normaal*. Roughly translated, it means, "Just act normal, that's crazy enough" or "Calm down."

Some expats here interpret this negatively, as societal pressure to maintain the status quo, to resign oneself to being average and to not want more. In fact, it's about accepting yourself for who you are. Life isn't Pinterest-perfect, and no one expects you to be perfect. It's about recognizing that you don't have to try so hard. The Dutch value authenticity and genuineness. They understand the messiness and imperfections of life.

And when it comes to parenting, *doe maar gewoon* is all about doing the best you can. Keep it real!

before the preschool admissions officers ask him, "So what have you done with the first thirty-six months of your life?" (This is assuming we might move back to the San Francisco Bay area.)

Being an expat mother brought an unexpected kinship with other foreigners living in the Netherlands whose native language happens to be English: British, Canadians, Australians and New Zealanders. In any case, we're "all English," according to the Dutch. *Zij is Engels* (She is English) is often how I'm introduced by (older) Dutch people. Intent on shaking off my feelings of loneliness and culture shock and my creeping awareness that I was turning into a desperate housewife, I started a blog, *Finding Dutchland*, about my experiences as an American expat mom in the Netherlands. Blogging seemed like a great way to combine my passions – writing, photography and family. It was also an honest attempt to connect with other *Engels* expats and a virtual portfolio of who I am. If people liked what they saw and read, perhaps they would want to be my friend.

I was slow to warm to the Dutch way of parenting. Raised on equal parts Catholic guilt and immigrant work ethic, the Dutch approach seemed a bit too easy-going, self-centered and lazy to me. I viewed with suspicion the midwife-assisted births, ideally at home and non-medicated. The Dutch didn't send their toddlers to music lessons or academic-enrichment programs, or worry about getting them into the right nursery school. What was wrong with them?

A year into motherhood I stumbled upon an article claiming that Dutch children were the happiest kids in the world, according to UNICEF. How true was this? Were they really that happy?

Deeply ingrained in the American psyche is the pursuit of happiness. We strive for perfect parenting, believing that being our children's twenty-four-hour playmates and constant supervisors will win us this coveted prize.

And an added jibe: Dutch parents were accomplishing this en masse and with a lot less effort. Maybe I just needed to calm down, and look at what the Dutch were doing. What if parenthood could actually be *fun*?

I became fascinated by what the parents around me were doing and started to analyze the differences between their and my approach. And I befriended the local children, who enjoyed stopping by to play with my son, the only baby on our block. One night, I decided to write my observations – "The Eight Secrets of Dutch Kids, the Happiest Kids in the World," my first attempt to be part of the mommy-sphere. My blog piece went viral, resonating with parents around the world.

Today, I'm frantically preparing for Julius' third birthday party in full Californian overachieving-mommy mode. (Since both my husband and our first son share the same name, I'm going to refer to our son as Julius to avoid confusion.) Apart from Dutch relatives, the guests include expats with children of around Julius' age. They, too, love the laid-back parenting philosophy here. These recovering workaholics are learning to appreciate the part-time work culture in Holland that is a viable option for even the most ambitious. And, like me, they rave about the benefits.

I'm busy with last-minute preparations – adding garnishes to the artisanal pizza, frying up homemade egg rolls, squeezing a bit more lime juice into the guacamole and preparing the Vietnamese beef-noodle salad. Maybe the *Mickey Mouse Clubhouse* paraphernalia and the dessert buffet consisting of a two-tiered fondant cake, red velvet cupcakes, chocolate truffles and Italian shortbread cookies give away the fact that I'm not a native. I try to integrate, but I am still prone to trying to be the domestic goddess.

Bram shakes his head in amusement, and my in-laws seem overwhelmed by all the effort I've made. My mother-in-law doesn't understand why I'm doing so much. But I find it impossible to shake off the idea that the more time, effort and thought I put into my child's birthday party, the more I prove my love for him. Yet it's exhausting, and I'm not even sure my son really appreciates it. The Dutch kids' parties we've been to are simple, down-to-earth affairs reserved for immediate family and maybe neighbors, where each guest gets one slice of cake and the adults sit in a circle, chatting politely for three hours while the children run around playing games.

Dutch birthdays, and most other celebrations, are more about celebrating togetherness. Our guests start by congratulating the parents and grandparents of the birthday boy, as well as the child. The Dutch expect you to congratulate everyone in the room. Needless to say, when I first came across this tradition, I found it a bit odd. Eventually, I started to appreciate this cultural idiosyncrasy. Like the custom of bringing in a treat for your classmates or treating your coworkers at the office to cake on your birthday, it's more about giving than receiving. I like that.

My son runs up to me, and says, "Cake, Mama." It's time for the birthday songs. The four-and-under crowd gathers round as the cake is placed before Julius. The first song is "Happy Birthday," sung in English, followed by the Dutch version, *Lang zal hij leven* (Long shall he live). I prefer the Dutch one, as it ends in "Hip, hip, hip, hoorah!" and the birthday boy raises his hands in a gesture of victory.

As Julius blows out his three birthday candles, I can't help but think to myself, *he's growing up happy.*

Meanwhile, Michele is living in Amsterdam's village metropolis . . .

Just as Rina and I are setting out on our journey to work out just what makes Dutch kids so happy, I have one of those days that exemplifies my new life here. It's a bright spring day and I'm up at the allotments just outside Amsterdam's ring road. Allotments, or *volkstuinen*, are Holland's equivalent to a community garden. Our complex has around three hundred separate plots upon which amateur gardeners can build wood cabins or greenhouses and grow anything from dahlias to cherry tomatoes. The allotments here resemble those back home in the UK, though they are much larger in scale and taken more seriously. I come here almost every weekend between April and October.

The birds are singing; one of them is calling out an insistent "cha-wee, cha-wee, cha-wee." I'm bent double, pulling grass out of my strawberry and raspberry patch with a metal claw. Six feet away on the unkempt lawn, my ten-year-old son, Benjamin, and his friend Floris are helping my Dutch husband, Martijn, reassemble the trampoline that has been in storage for the winter. The two boys are working well together, putting all their strength into stretching the springs between the canvas and the frame. My eight-year-old daughter, Ina, called her best friend, Tijn, earlier this morning and set off on her scooter to play at his house.

It's a peaceful, harmonious scene, complete with sunshine and daffodils. When the trampoline is ready, the boys take turns jumping on it. I joke about Floris' weight, checking if he's under the maximum the canvas can take. At eleven years old, he's almost as tall as me, one of those strapping Dutch lads with enormous feet. My half-English son looks like a dwarf next to him. They say it's growth hormones in the milk, but I suspect genes have more to do with it.

Two hours later, I'm still weeding. It's a labor-intensive endeavor, and mice have dug tunnels under the plants. The Dutch are outdoorsy types and love their allotments. Most of them spend a lot more time at theirs than I do. There are five or six large complexes within ten minutes of my house. Unlike British allotments, which tend to feature a few rows of vegetables and a rickety shed, the Dutch go all out and build luxury cabins with solar panels, running water and gas. Since they all love camping, their allotments become mini weekend campsites, and they often spend the night. The complex is dotted with tanned pensioners sunning themselves on folding chairs, children playing with water and mud, and dedicated gardeners, headscarved and bent-backed. There is a football pitch, a sandbox and a playground for the kids and a large canteen serving beer and snacks for the adults. On the weekends, there are card tournaments, bingo and sing-alongs.

Ben and Floris are taking turns lying on their bellies across the trampoline. They talk constantly, inventing and reinventing whatever fantasy they are in – they are rockets, astronauts, swimmers, Olympic divers, acrobats; they are in a weightless world with no gravity; they have superpowers; they can do seventeen back flips; they have been kidnapped and taken to a tree hut; they somersault out of the tree hut and are back on the trampoline. They tell each other jokes, some even making fun of the right-wing extremist Geert Wilders and giggling at simple puns. Ben chatters excitedly about yesterday's Saturday drama club, still relishing the fun he had backstage between performances.

I ask Floris whether he doesn't have to review today for the tests coming up at school. He looks at me in surprise. *Of course not, what a peculiar thought!* his face seems to suggest. The reason I inquire is because the boys are in the process of moving from elementary to high school (there are no middle schools in the Netherlands), and I know from Ben that Floris is on the borderline between two different tracks. But neither of the boys mentions the impending exams. Nothing seems to be further from their minds. Today is Sunday, and from Tuesday to Thursday the boys will be taking their final elementary school exams, the Cito. These standardized tests measure a child's academic abilities in order to stream them into the broad range of secondary or high schools – from academic to technical, vocational or manual. Secondary school in the Netherlands is equivalent to middle through high school in the US, for children aged 12 to 18. In other words, this pivotal exam may influence the rest of a child's life and their possible career choices.

To be honest, I have been feeling rather nervous about the Cito. Martijn and I are pretty sure our son is not going to do particularly well. Though Ben's previous results have been good – he even skipped a grade – he is easily distracted and doesn't perform well on multiple-choice exams. He tends to just choose the first option that looks as if it might be right, without reading the others. In the few practice tests he's done, he's gotten most of the answers wrong! If it was up to me, I'd be reviewing with him and coaching him, as I would if we lived in Britain. But his teacher, Cinthya, a calm woman the same age as me – in her early forties – has specifically asked me not to.

"You don't want to put him under any strain," she cautioned, as if putting a child under any kind of pressure was the worst thing a parent could do.

It was more of an imperative than a polite suggestion. And I have learned not to mess with Dutch women. These days, I don't so much pick my battles as head for the hills. Dutch women are bigger, stronger and a lot more assertive than I am. While the men seem like gentle giants, the women are fierce. What's more, Cinthya seemed to know what she was doing and had everything under control. So I ended up deciding, against my gut instincts, to trust her.

Ben has already handed in the list of the ten secondary schools he'd like to go to, in order of preference. When we attended the schools' open houses, he was encouraged to pick the ones he felt most comfortable at. After that, Cinthya discussed his choices with him. As parents, we were involved only as advisors, relegated to the back seat. Ben read up on the different schools and their teaching methods, discussed their reputations with older friends and looked up the distances he would have to travel.

His first choice is a very modern school with an emphasis on the liberal arts, with film studies and drama on the curriculum. His second is the old-fashioned college preparatory high school his grandfather attended, again partly because it does drama studies. Unlike his parents, our boy's a born thesp. Even as a baby, he'd play to the crowd, putting on a show before he could even talk. In fact, Ben is a lot more interested in the school musical, in which he has a leading role – the culmination of *his* primary school ambitions – than in his exams.

Martijn tells me that when he was eleven it was his Amsterdam elementary school that decided which high school he should attend. Parental preference, it seems, has never been a major influence here. This must be what people mean when they call the Netherlands "a child-centered society." It's the child who has to go to the school, after all. Sadly, American-style "concerted cultivation" parenting practices are creeping into the country's affluent pockets, and this worries me. Parents who prepare their children academically and hire private tutors have lost sight of the value of the Dutch school system, which is in favor of placing the child under minimal stress. Luckily, in my part of town, there is still more emphasis on what the child wants and what the teacher thinks is best than on what parents might aspire to.

In June, we'll find out which school our son will be going to. We're spoiled for choice – there are twenty-four that offer the type of schooling thought suitable for him. All the ones we visited looked fine to me. Trusting the child to make their own choice is a lot less stressful for the parent. A new "matching system" has just been imported from New York. You pick ten schools and are guaranteed a place at one of them, or so the theory goes. The system aims to place the children in a school as close to the top of their list as possible. But it's the first year, so we are guinea pigs.

Before, there was a lottery system. Since the spots available at the half dozen most popular schools were – and still are – limited, a child would either get into their first choice of school (and most did) or go through a clearing system to find a place elsewhere. The Dutch adore lottery systems, perhaps because they rule out nepotism and favoritism. The Dutch are also oddly averse to meritocratic procedures. There are no interviews, and places are not allocated according to grades. This is alien to me, as I come from a culture where getting the highest grades is seen as a fast track to success in life. When I was a child, my fear of failing exams became all-encompassing and I began to have panic attacks. I would throw up in the bathrooms beforehand. I remember once getting up and running out of a math exam, my face streaked with tears. The headmaster caught up with me at the school gates.

Looking back, I can see that I internalized my parents' ambitions for me. They had moved into the catchment area of a grammar school so that I could get the best kind of state education available. I was a good student, a high achiever, and terrified of displeasing my mother. At Ben's age, I was also a competitive swimmer, training every day and often traveling around the country with my teammates to compete on the weekends. I used to throw up in the toilets at the pools, too, terrified of not improving on my personal best. My childhood was one big competition and I had to be the best every time.

When I moved to the Netherlands eleven years ago, I wasn't thinking about schools. Thirty-seven weeks pregnant, I was planning on joining Martijn in Amsterdam for the duration of my six-month paid maternity leave, and then heading back to London and the job I loved.[1] I was an ambitious young workaholic pursuing a career in publishing. I pictured my child going to daycare in northwest London; I'd worry about schools later. My weekend commuter marriage across the North Sea had worked fabulously so far; I assumed – naively, as it turned out – that it would work when we were parents, too. My own father had often been away working on oil rigs during my early childhood years. I figured fathers were optional in child-rearing – more fool me.

Reality soon hit when I found myself at home with a screaming baby. Looking after a baby takes up a whole lot of time and energy, and there I was, planning to return to a full-on job and the stresses of London. I started looking into the practicalities of raising my child in Amsterdam, and it was clear there was a whole stack of advantages. You could cycle anywhere in the city, so there'd be no stuffy underground trains or overcrowded, run-down buses to contend with. Dutch parents seemed laid-back, small children ran about happily – even in restaurants! My sister-in-law's children were polite and friendly, and there was a unified state-school system, so no terrifying gulf between public and private, between the haves and the have-nots. That was a huge draw. Maybe it would be a good thing to raise my child here? I decided to bite the bullet and stay in Amsterdam.

Whenever I visited London, I'd catch up with my friends, and I soon became aware of the differences in our lives as new mothers. At first, they weren't so huge: There were crèches (daycare centers) and nannies in the Netherlands, too, for example. But as the children grew older and started school, it was clear that the two countries operated very differently. The *Telegraph* recently estimated that, in the UK, it costs £600,000 (about $750,000) to privately educate two children from nursery age through the equivalent of high school and then send them to university for three years.[2] We could never have afforded that, and neither can many of my London friends. One option for them is to move into the catchment area of a good state school, and some of them have done that.

My friend Helen, who lives in Surrey and now commutes into central London, told me she feels guilty about not having been able to provide the "best education" for her children. "If you don't go private, you haven't done literally everything you could," she confided. She looked at me a little enviously when I said that in the Netherlands, the only option is the state-school system. Private schools generally only exist for expats, namely, the British School, the American School, and the International School.

My friend Selma, who lives in affluent Knightsbridge, complained that her children's private school expected too much of its students. The headmistress had asked to speak to her about her youngest boy, saying that she was "afraid her son was falling behind academically." The problem was that her five-year-old did not yet know his times tables by heart. Selma was horrified that her son was being branded a failure at such a young age. In the Netherlands, children don't start to learn reading, writing and arithmetic until the age of six; until then, the focus is on structured play.

And these are just two examples. Many people back home have issues with schools and childcare that we just don't experience in the Netherlands. I know it's not comparing like with like – Amsterdam is minuscule compared with New York or London. Of course, living in a smaller city makes life with children easier, but the differences go further than being purely a matter of scale. American and British parents seem to exert much more control over their children's lives and spend much of their scarce free time taxiing their kids around – children just aren't allowed out on their own. But who in their right mind would let a child wander freely, with hysteria-inducing headlines of mass shootings, terrorist attacks, kidnappings and pedophiles? The Dutch don't have a "gutter press," so even though there are real threats in the Netherlands, too, the threats are not blown up out of all proportion.

Many big-city schools in the US and UK operate on security levels similar to those you'd find in Dutch high-security prisons. And American parents are simply terrified of anyone coming into their child's school after yet more mass shootings. There are metal detectors at the entrance to a north London state primary school one of my friends sends his children to. This would never happen in the Netherlands. Anyone can walk into a Dutch school. This doesn't mean there are killers wandering in; it's that the perceived threat is kept in perspective.

When Selma told me she just didn't have the energy to organize her children's social lives, I looked at her in shock. I couldn't believe this was something people did. She told me that simply playing in the park was not what British city children did. She said they wanted expensive entertainments, day trips and planned activities. At home, they expect the newest video games, surround-sound home cinemas, and all the rest. She recounted having taken one of her sons and a friend bowling, then driven them back to her house. The friend asked to call his mother and be picked up after half an hour because there was nothing to do. When did children forget how to play?

Several intelligent, ambitious British friends of mine have put their careers on hold in order to cope with the demands of modern parenting. The pressure is extreme. Parents are so anxious to give their children the best start in life, they've become caught up in a vicious cycle of perfectionism. Our generation is the first since the Second World War that hasn't become materially better off than their parents. Being top of the class, graduating with a first-class degree, playing a musical instrument to college-level proficiency or qualifying to compete in the Olympics won't make the rest of your life any easier, or guarantee success and happiness in the future. We know this. Yet we're pushing our children harder, encouraging them to achieve more and more in an attempt to ensure their future financial safety and well-being.

Schools in the Netherlands, on the other hand, do not put young Dutch children, or their parents, under pressure to succeed. It isn't that they are immune to pressure, it's that there is less pressure. The children enjoy their time in the classroom. And when they aren't at school, they're out playing. Isn't that what we should be aspiring to – that our children enjoy being at school? For them to know how to play? But why is it that Dutch parents don't seem to be as worried about their children's academic performance?

To get a few initial ideas, I ask the mothers at my monthly book group. I'm the only non-Dutch mom; the seven other mothers form a perfect, if unscientific, research group. Their children range in age from six to twelve years old. I tell them I am working on a book on childhood happiness and ask them to tell me what comes into their heads when I ask them why Dutch kids are happy. "Happiness is not having the most but accepting what you have. Our children accept they won't be the best footballer in the world. They are resilient," says one. "Dutch children have a voice and join in the conversation," says another. "Parents can work part-time, so they have more time for their kids," says a third. And then, the most obvious: "Children are free to play. They can play outside on their own."

The lives of my London friends seem radically different from our relaxed life in Amsterdam. Right from the start, I've been won over by the Dutch way of parenting. Unlike Rina, I didn't struggle with my cultural baggage but tried to shake off my British values and integrate. Despite my belief that the Netherlands is the perfect place to bring up kids, it would be wrong to call it paradise here. It hasn't been that easy to integrate and let's face it: The weather's shit.

———

After spending the afternoon at the allotment, we cycle back home and stop for ice cream on the edge of the park near our house. Ben spots his sister, Ina, in the distance. She's playing football in a group of eight or nine children, all under the age of ten. Her best friend, Tijn, is with her, but of course, neither of his parents are in tow. Ben decides to surprise Ina once he's finished his ice cream, but we get talking, lose sight of her and then she's gone. As we walk back, we spot her racing along the pavement on her space scooter, carrying her jacket. She's on her way home, too. We'd asked her to be back by half past four. We run to meet her, arriving just in time to open the door for her. "Phew!" she sighs, feigning exhaustion but looking rosy-cheeked. "I just played in the park for four and a half hours in one go."

I am proud of her. She arranged her own playdate in the morning, played in the park all afternoon and came home at the agreed time. She's a tomboy; you only have to give her a ball and she'll kick it happily for hours. But still, if I let her, she would glue herself to the iPad or the Wii for hours, like most kids these days. Watching other Dutch parents has taught me to encourage unsupervised outdoor play and gradually give her a longer and longer leash, something we'll discuss later in the book. Away from their parents, children don't need constant attention, they just get on with it. It works for both parties. Like Rina, I want this kind of childhood for my children.

2

Mothering the Mother

In which Rina explores Dutch birthing practices

As I anticipate the birth of my second child, I am anxious but resolute. I am going to give birth the way I want to. My birth plan is simple. All I ask is to be sufficiently drugged during the delivery to alleviate the pain and to have another healthy baby in my arms while I convalesce in the hospital for a couple of days.

At the upper end of the millennial generation (those between the ages of eighteen and thirty-five), I've become used to customizing practically everything about my life: my hair and clothes, what I eat, my exercise routine, social networks and lifestyle. I aspire to be different and well informed – just like the eighty-odd million other millennials who grew up as a "special snowflake." I have researched down to the smallest detail my prenatal care, the birth and my postpartum recovery and come up with a custom-made plan. This, I believe, is a measure of how much I love my baby and how much I want the absolute best for him.

Except there is one major hurdle. I am pregnant and will give birth to my baby in the Netherlands.

"The Dutch tradition is to give birth at home, assisted by a midwife and without any pain relief," explains Mariska, my sixty-three-year-old Dutch neighbor. She's over at my house for coffee. Mariska is a retired nurse and both her parents were physicians, so she knows what she's talking about. "The Dutch believe that pregnancy and labor are normal events rather than a medical condition," she says.

The no-nonsense attitude to parenting here starts from the beginning, even before a child is born. Unlike much of the rest of the world (the US and the UK are prime examples), where pregnancy is pervasively medicalized, the Dutch see pregnancy and delivery as just another part of life, and home births are encouraged as much as possible. The exceptions are women considered to be at high risk of serious complications. It's a *nuchter* (sober and sensible) approach, and the Dutch pride themselves on being sober and sensible. For the Dutch, giving birth in the comfort of their own home is the most logical way to welcome a new member of the family.

The concept of "home" as we comprehend it today hasn't always existed. According to some historians, the word *home* acquired its emotional connotations in the Netherlands in the seventeenth century – a hundred years earlier than elsewhere in Europe.[1] Wealthy and urbanized, the Dutch middle class were the first to be able to afford a modest house purely for the nuclear family – Mom, Dad and the kids. This was the first time the house evolved into a home exclusively revolving around family life, with the children firmly at the center. The physical space where these Dutch families spent time together became associated with comfort, domesticity, intimacy and refuge.

"Did you know that I gave birth to my youngest son, Tjerk, in what is now your bedroom, and during a snowstorm?" says Mariska, after taking a sip of her coffee. "That was twenty-five years ago." I catch her looking around our living room, reminiscing about what it was like all those years ago. She and her husband were the original owners of this cottage. When all three of her sons left the nest, the family divided the property and sold the cottage, and Mariska and her husband built their dream home on the remaining land.

I had thought I leaned a bit crunchy. After all, I spent my high school and college years in Berkeley, California, the birthplace of the hippie movement. I'm all for having my children sing "Kumbaya" around the campfire, feeding them organic foods and taking them out for regular country walks. But giving birth at home? With no pain relief, and no doctor within a few seconds' reach? Could this Dutch approach really result in happier moms and happier kids?

"Were you not scared giving birth at home, and during a snowstorm?" I ask.

"Of course not. If anything had gone wrong, we would have been able to make it to the hospital in time. It's nearby," Mariska responds. In the Netherlands, home birth is part of an integrated health care system in which midwives and doctors work closely together. And in case of an emergency, because the country is so densely populated, the nearest hospital is usually just a few miles away. "We Dutch women are strong. We can bear the pain of childbirth. I had a midwife with me, and I didn't need an epidural, or any other drugs. I was in my own bed, with my own duvet, in my own bedroom, with my husband by my side. No strangers, no bright lights, no clanging hospital equipment."

Mariska notices the look of misgiving and reluctance on my face. She smiles and, as if letting me in on a secret, states, "As a matter of fact, we really give birth at home because it's *gezellig*."

Ah, that's it! I should have known that this word, which has no equivalent in English, had something to do with it. *Gezellig* (pronounced *ggggheh-sell-ig*, with a hard, guttural *g* that sounds like someone clearing their throat) evokes feelings of coziness, warmth, belonging, love, happiness, security, contentment, safety and companionship. It's similar to the Danish *hygge*, another untranslatable word that encompasses the feelings of coziness and taking pleasure from the presence of gentle, soothing things.

It's the feeling you get when you're sitting by the fire surrounded by loved ones, drinking hot chocolate and eating marshmallows. It has its root in the Dutch word *gezel*, which means "companion" or "friend," and it's about fostering bonds with your loved ones. How *gezellig* a place – or a gathering, a party, a meal, a playdate; really, anything that is part of human social experience – is is a key indicator of how enjoyable it is and how much those there appreciate it. It seems an odd adjective to choose to describe childbirth, though. "Painful," "life altering," "unpredictable," "transformative" – these are the words that come to my mind when I think about childbirth, not a word evoking warm family togetherness.

Mariska is not the only one who mentions a *gezellig* home birth – I've heard it from others, even expats. My South African friend Elma is a fan of the Dutch idea of home births. "On the second day after my home delivery with Stella, I was already up on my feet and making breakfast for the whole family. It was so nice. Lovely, actually," she tells me. "To me, it was more about being at home, surrounded by family and having an awesome midwife. None of that stress often associated with hospitals; no rushing around and much less anxiety. The intimacy and togetherness of giving birth at home – I'm a bit embarrassed to say this – was *gezellig*."

For my friends Rob and Gowri, a Dutch-Singaporean couple, Gowri giving birth at home when they had their second child was a way to reassert their control. Written by Rob, the birth announcement read, "In the warm surroundings of our home, Gowri gave birth to Nikki's lovely little sister, Kira." I couldn't resist saying the words out loud: "in the warm surroundings of our home." There it is in a nutshell: Giving birth at home is *gezellig*.

Ironically, almost every other highly developed country considers giving birth too risky a matter to routinely happen at home. Yet, according to Save the Children's sixteenth annual State of the World's Mothers report, the Netherlands is among the safest places in the world to give birth and be born; it ranks sixth. The US and the UK failed to make the top ten, coming in at thirty-third and twenty-fourth, respectively.[2]

The Netherlands, with its long-standing tradition of midwifery care, also has a dramatically lower rate of C-section births. For many women in the rest of the developed world, the likelihood of having a C-section has become astonishingly high: In the US, it's approximately one in every three births, while in the UK it's one in four.[3] In the Netherlands, it's fewer than one in ten. When I list these statistics, I can't help but think of Ricky Lake's 2008 documentary, *The Business of Being Born*, where she explores the modern medicalization of childbirth and the rise of C-sections.

In the Netherlands about 25 percent of births happen at home. That is the highest rate relative to all the other rich countries, although it's probably still lower than they would like it to be. Back home in America, home births or out-of-hospital births are still rare, comprising only 1.36 percent of births. Home births, despite the slight observed increase by the Centers for Disease Control and Prevention, remain an unregulated, underground practice.[4]

Before singing the praises of home births in Holland, it's crucial to list the ways that make it such a safe alternative for expecting moms. *Slate*'s article "Why the Netherlands Is a Red Herring in the Home Birth Debate" brings it home.[5] Dutch midwives receive much more formal and professional training than their US counterparts. Their closest American equivalents, known as certified nurse midwives (CNM), usually do not participate in home births. Rather, it's lay midwives – certified professional midwives or direct-entry midwives – who attend the births. Furthermore, there is an integrated system of care and communication between Dutch midwives and obstetricians, creating a safe environment in which to give birth regardless of whether at home, a birth center or a hospital. And finally, there is an established transfer system to get laboring women to a nearby hospital should emergencies arise.

Birthing tips from Dutch moms

- Consider having a *pijn-is-fijn* (pain is good) delivery. For some, labor pain can be a positive experience that pumps your body full of endorphins and gives you a natural high that enables you to bond with your baby. However, if you aren't able to give birth without pain relief, remember that what's most important is a healthy baby and mommy.

- It can be very *gezellig* to have a midwife-assisted birth at home. If conditions allow, don't be afraid of giving birth at home, especially if it's your second baby. You will feel more comfortable and relaxed in familiar surroundings. And, if necessary, you can always make your way to a hospital.

- Aim to have a *bevalling die bevalt* (a delivery that pleases you). Look at all the childbirth options and decide which will suit you best. Light candles, play music and hire a doula. However, keep in mind that medical emergencies may arise.

A modern Dutch birth

Having been in and out of the hospital over the summer with preterm contractions, at thirty-six weeks I am woken by a gush of water trickling down my legs. Because of being a high-risk pregnancy due to some complications, I'm under the supervision of an obstetrician. With an overnight bag already packed and wiping the sleep away from our eyes, my husband and I hand Julius over to the babysitter and head to the local hospital.

The nurse confirms that my water has broken, and I am transferred to a private triage room. In walks Dr. Jan, a handsome obstetrician with classic Dutch looks: He's tall, blond, blue-eyed and fit. He speaks English with a British accent, having spent some time studying at Oxford. It's impossible not to be charmed by him. Dr. Jan tells me that the body intuitively knows how to give birth to a baby and instructs me to take a long, hot shower and to walk around to try to move things along.

Naturally, the moment he walks out of the room, the intensity and frequency of my contractions increases. My husband holds my hand, and we watch the clock. The loud, obnoxious American in me is revealed. I shout and swear, which brings the midwife into the room. She gives me a crash refresher course in Lamaze breathing exercises – hee, hoo, hee, hoo – and outlines the Dutch philosophy of *pijn-is-fijn* (pain is good): Pain is a necessary part of the process and helps the mother bond with her baby after birth.

Before I know it, I'm whisked into the delivery room. It is too late to have an epidural. Dr. Jan reappears and takes over. I'm officially in love. Apparently, he asked to attend the birth, even though his shift had ended. I have a huge smile on my face, in spite of everything; it's as if I have a silly schoolgirl crush on him. My husband is also enamored by his bedside manner.

"You need to breathe," he gently reminds me. "Follow me. Hee. Hoo. Hee. Hoo."

In the final moments I decide to let go of all the pain. As my husband holds one hand and Sylvie, the delivery nurse, the other, I follow the charming doctor's cadence of "hee, hoo, hee, hoo." Finally, at 5:39 PM, Matteo arrives.

Sylvie continues to make me feel special. She says to me, "Having an unmedicated birth is like running a marathon. You should be very proud of yourself."

While I am thanking Dr. Jan, he says with his Mr. Congeniality smile, "No. You did all the work. Congratulations on going Dutch."

I finally understand that the Dutch approach to childbirth isn't really about having a natural, unmedicated delivery and embracing pain. It's about allowing a mother to feel tenacious, strong and fierce. Going

Dutch at birth means surrounding yourself with supportive, compassionate care providers, enabling you to do it naturally and on your own or, if necessary, with pain relief. It's beginning to dawn on me that the Dutch have internalized the adage "Happy moms have happy kids." By allowing women to give birth in a supportive, loving environment, they provide moms-to-be with the emotional fortitude and support to make childbirth a positive experience. And by viewing pregnancy and delivery as natural processes, they avoid the panicked, medical, emergency mood often found in the US and the UK.

Michele's first Dutch birth

A couple of days after arriving in the Netherlands, at thirty-seven weeks pregnant, I confidently handed my British birth plan to my local Dutch midwife. "Oh no," she said, shaking her head. "You'll be giving birth at home in the usual way." It was as if I didn't have any other option. She glanced at my notes: I was requesting nitrous oxide during contractions, and meperidine, if necessary; no epidural. "There'll be no pain relief," she said curtly. "Here's a list of things you'll need to buy."

The list included wooden blocks to raise the bed, plastic sheeting and navel clamps. The things on it seemed medieval. Of course, back in London I'd been reading books like *Birth and Beyond* and *A Child Is Born*, reading up on Mumsnet and comparing notes with pregnant friends, but somehow I'd failed to do any research into how the Dutch approached childbirth. What they did when they could was give birth at home. It was taken for granted. My husband assured me that a home birth was perfectly normal.

It had certainly never occurred to me that, rather than having an overnight bag packed, we'd be ordering a special maternity kit and putting wooden blocks under the bed so the midwife wouldn't hurt her back. When they arrived, we stacked everything – the hydrophilic wipes (whatever they were), the navel clamps and mattress protectors – in a neat pile in the corner of the bedroom. The due date came and went. I jumped up and down on the spot, scrubbed every last nook and cranny of the bathroom with a toothbrush, finished off some embroidery I'd started as a child and somehow brought with me, chopped down some small willow trees in the back garden, drove along bumpy country lanes, ate curry, had sex: all to no avail.

When I was two weeks overdue, the midwife summoned me to her office, where, my knees splayed on a plastic-covered couch, she tried to stimulate the birth by sweeping my cervix manually. The procedure hurt and reminded me of veterinary science, but it didn't work. I was sent to the hospital to be induced. I can't say I wasn't relieved.

In which Rina discovers the magic of the Dutch maternity nurse

The joy of welcoming a new baby in Holland continues once everyone is safely at home. I was looking forward to taking Matteo home, not least because I knew that waiting for us would be our own personal maternity nurse. Here in the Low Countries, getting mothers back on their feet after delivery seems to be a matter of national interest. A maternity nurse known as a *kraamverzorgster* is provided for all new mothers, regardless of their income, to offer postpartum care and support for eight to ten days after the birth (more if medically necessary). Rhada is a mother of four, soft around the edges and with a hearty, contagious laugh. She also happens to be a breastfeeding consultant.

The Dutch recognize that entry into motherhood, especially for first-time moms, can be a bumpy road, replete with unanticipated life changes and emotions ranging from bliss to isolation and, in some cases, depression. American moms of my generation are encouraged to focus on scripting and having the "perfect birth," whether it's a midwife-assisted home birth or a fully medicated hospital delivery. There's not enough emphasis on the realities they might face once the baby arrives – breastfeeding problems, exhaustion, anxiety, sleep

Beschuit met muisjes

Beschuit met muisjes is the traditional snack served in the Netherlands to celebrate the homecoming of a newborn. A *beschuit* is a round breakfast rusk, buttered and sprinkled with *muisjes* (little mice) – aniseed coated in sugar. Aniseed is believed to stimulate the flow of breastmilk. The *muisjes* are generally blue for a baby boy and pink for a girl. And, although the Dutch tend not to be particularly royalist, when the queen has a child, orange *muisjes* are produced to mark the occasion.

deprivation and the rollercoaster ride of emotions. In the Netherlands, the *kraamverzorgster* is on hand to help.

Michele and her family are at my house to welcome baby Matteo and, naturally, we are swapping birth stories and sharing the experiences we had with the maternity nurses who looked after us.

"After I had my first baby, I could hardly even look after myself, let alone myself and the baby. I'd never changed a baby's diaper before and had no idea how to do any of the practical stuff: breastfeeding, bathing or even dressing my baby," confesses Michele as she watches Ina, her daughter, cuddling Matteo. "My first maternity nurse gave me a crash course in baby care, showing me how to do all that stuff. She also shopped, cooked and cleaned, and looked after all the visitors, making hot drinks and biscuits for them. Basically, I had full-time help for three weeks."

Michele's story is similar to that of many first-time mothers in Holland. The maternity nurse comes in to teach the new mother basic parenting skills – how to breastfeed, how to soothe and bathe the baby – as well as looking after the mother, making sure any stitches she may have had are healing, and offering practical help. She is trained to recognize signs of trouble in a newborn (jaundice, for example) or a new mother (any postpartum complications or indications of depression). She will also take over household chores like vacuuming, cleaning the bathrooms, preparing home-cooked meals and looking after guests who come to congratulate the parents and meet the baby.

"Who would like some *beschuit met muisjes*?" Rhada has just come from the kitchen bringing a tray. Everyone happily takes one.

"Come on, Julius, let's play ball outside," she says. "Let's see who can get outside the fastest."

"Me, me!" screams Julius. "I'm the winner, I'm the winner!" The two rush out to the garden, Rhada deliberately two steps behind the toddler.

Seeing Rhada taking care of me, my baby and my family brought back memories for Michele. "When I had Ina, Ben was only two and a half. I was able to get back on my feet more quickly, so I only had one week of maternity help. But since I was juggling a toddler and a baby, I really appreciated the help," she says.

Our maternity nurses were not unique in the help they gave. This is from Dutch writer Abdelkader Benali's Facebook profile:

> We have just said goodbye to our maternity nurse, Audrey. She was brilliant. "If you think no milk will come, no milk will come," she said. She gave us so much confidence in dealing with Amber. She taught my wife the rugby grip and the tiger-on-wood grip, and advised, "Don't use baby talk with Amber." She was dedicated, professional and nice. Sometimes you get lucky. We got lucky with Audrey.

"What exactly are the rugby grip and the tiger-on-wood grip?" I messaged him, wanting to know more.

"It's a way of holding the child so that they are comfortable and secure. The rugby hold is the way the rugby player holds the ball, never going to give it back, in the crook of the arm. The tiger-on-wood is holding the child on your arm, like it's a tiger lying lazily along a tree branch. It's important to have different ways of holding the child to avoid your arms and neck getting stiff."

I asked what a typical day with Audrey was like. "She was great. She showed up the first morning at home and started to encourage Saida to breastfeed, telling her to believe that the milk would come. She showed Saida how to position her breast correctly and how to massage herself. She told us how to interpret the baby's crying or yawning. I liked her style – she was very matter-of-fact, very open and positive."

"Did she surprise you in any way?"

"We were pleasantly surprised that she was so inspiring, really giving us confidence, telling us we shouldn't despair when the baby cried, and that breastfeeding and cuddling the baby were the best way to bond," he replied.

Being once again under the care of the maternity nurse makes me think about how different the postpartum experience is here. Elsewhere in the Western world, new moms and dads are expected to cope with their newborn with little or no support. In Britain, assuming that there are no complications and mom and baby are in good health, they can be discharged as early as six hours after the birth. The rationale is that home is a better place to recuperate, but some compare the process to a conveyor belt: British women spend less time in the hospital after giving birth than in any other European country.[6]

In Britain, Michele tells me, although a midwife will make several home visits in the first ten days, unless you are having difficulties, you won't have a daily checkup. Curious to know more, I ask Michele's friend Leilah, a lawyer who lives in southeast London, about her experiences. Leilah is a mom of three, the youngest nine months old.

"There isn't much postnatal support in the UK. There are a few visits from the health visitor, and that's it," she comments. "I paid for a night nanny with my third, but it's really expensive. I think more support would be amazing!"

American moms fare even worse. They are nudged out of the hospital within a day or two. The only standard postpartum follow-up in the US is an appointment with the obstetrician at six weeks, long after most of the aches and pains from the birth have subsided. Mothers are expected to bounce back to normal immediately after childbirth, without the support, pampering and rest offered by the Dutch system. They have to rely on their own personal network – their mother, aunts, sisters, friends, church members or neighbors – for help. Or, if they have deeper pockets, they can hire their own private maternity nurse or postpartum doula. But the reality is that there is a growing number of urban professional mothers in both America and Britain without a family network nearby, and with little or no experience of babies, who are left to fend for themselves.

While limited follow-up care might not cause any difficulties, in some instances serious problems may arise without anyone noticing. Postpartum depression affects one in every seven women and, despite greater awareness, many of these cases go unrecognized and the mother is left unsupported. In the Netherlands, the *kraamverzorgsters* screen for this. "Depression can occur during the postpartum period," Rhada says. "We're here to look after the mom's well-being and check her mood. If we see a mom suffering from possible postpartum depression, we urge her to get medical help."

"What happens if she doesn't seek help?" I ask Rhada.

"That has never happened, at least in my experience. The moms I have worked with are often grateful and relieved that someone is there to recognize and name what they are experiencing. There is an entire support network in place – their partner, their doctor, the midwife and me. There's no sense of shame but rather an openness about getting help."

The Dutch maternity nurse treats the mother and her infant as a single unit, and uses the postpartum period to gently mentor and support the mother. The main goal is to nurture a self-sufficient, confident mother who can provide a safe, calm environment for her contented baby.

It is important to be honest about what can happen in the postpartum period. The reality of motherhood in the early days is often not the idealized picture of a smiling, rested mom putting her feet up with a hot cup of tea, the baby happily asleep in a Moses basket. If mothers can get past the shame of acknowledging that adjusting to newfound motherhood is hard – the lack of sleep, difficulties with breastfeeding or bonding with the child – we can start talking openly about just how much help we really do need, and ask for it, as new mothers do here in the Netherlands. Giving birth the Dutch way does seem to create the best, most supportive environment for new mothers.

Dutch baby announcements

The Dutch announce the arrival of the newest member of the family with a certain flair. These are the three most common ways:

- "New baby" cards. The Dutch love to send out cards via snail mail to let everyone know of the arrival of their baby, the child's name and the times when visitors are welcome to drop by.

- Decorating the front of the house. The whole neighborhood will know a new baby has been born when they see a massive stork and pink or blue bunting in the front window.

- *Beschuit met muisjes*. Proud new dads bring *beschuit met muisjes* to their workplace to celebrate the birth of the new baby with their coworkers. Elder siblings take them to school to share with their classmates.

3

The Real Happiest Babies on the Block

Where Rina contemplates easy babies and good-enough parents

I'm rocking my newborn, Matteo, swaying back and forth in his great-grandfather's rocking chair. He's asleep on my chest. I can't help but think to myself, *He's such an easy baby*. I'm convinced that going Dutch from the start the second time around has contributed to his happy disposition.

I long to be like all the other Dutch moms around me, who look rested, basking in the glow and sense of warmth a new baby brings. I see these happy, relaxed women all around me – pushing their strollers over the cobblestones, taking leisurely walks along the canals, holding their babies close to their chest in baby carriers, or cycling around with an older baby securely fastened in a cargo bike. None look the least bit stressed or anxious about incorporating a newborn into their lives. They look as content and smile as easily as the blond little cherubs with them and, as for the babies, there is no sign of any tears or tantrums. The Dutch make parenting look easy.

I first caught a glimpse of Dutch parenting through my friends Roos and Daan, a stereotypically Dutch blond, blue-eyed couple, each of whom would tower over the average American or British male. They were the first to have a baby in our circle of friends. During a lunch date while I was pregnant with my first son, Julius, Roos would repeatedly exclaim, "Finn is such an *easy baby*! He is just *so easy*!" I would look down and smile at her three-month-old baby, who seemed to be content and would be gurgling away in his stroller. He would just lie there, looking up without a care in the world while his mom and I enjoyed a leisurely lunch outside.

I initially found the way Roos tossed around the word "easy" slightly irritating. From what I read on the mommy blogosphere, babies were anything but. And I couldn't help feeling a bit guilty that we were enjoying ourselves and relaxing rather than focusing exclusively on Finn.

Daan boasted to Bram about just how easy being a dad was. He would set Finn in the "box," a square wooden playpen ubiquitous in all Dutch households with young babies. This would leave Daan free to do his chores – check his email, do the laundry, vacuum or prepare a quick lunch. One time, he took a conference call for work for forty-five minutes in his upstairs office, leaving Finn in his box in the living room, staring into space, quiet and contented.

Roos and Daan didn't submit to the unrealistic demands of intensive parenting. They approached it with the aim of simply being a "good-enough parent." The underlying premise is straightforward: Keep calm. Doing your best is good enough.

The idea of the *good-enough mother* was first posited by British pediatrician and psychoanalyst Donald Winnicott in the 1950s. After studying thousands of mothers and their babies, he came to the enlightened conclusion that the way to be a good mother was to be a good-enough mother.[1] Being a perfect mother is neither possible nor desirable. As psychologist Dr. Jennifer Kunst writes:

> Winnicott's good-enough mother is sincerely preoccupied with being a mother. She pays attention to her baby. She provides a holding environment. She offers both physical and emotional care. She provides security. When she fails, she tries again. She weathers painful feelings. She makes sacrifices. Winnicott's good-enough mother is not so much a goddess; she is a gardener. She tends her baby with love, patience, effort and care.[2]

The Dutch take this to heart. They have a realistic perspective on parenthood and understand that they (and their children) are far from perfect. They are parents who live in the real world. That's not to say that they don't still struggle with the daily realities and messiness of life. But because they are more forgiving of their own imperfections and shortfalls, they're able to enjoy parenthood.

And no, the Dutch definitely do not care if little Sophie or Sem is a piano prodigy, a chess champion or an Instagram model famous by the age of two. There are no Baby Einstein DVDs being played, no black-and-white flash cards being used, and definitely no baby enrichment classes or baby gyms, at least not outside of the major cities. The Dutch aren't concerned about their babies being the smartest. They seem to just want them to be the easiest.

As if the universe was conspiring for me to parent like the Dutch the second time around, a headline in *New York* magazine, "Dutch Babies: Better than American Babies?," appeared on my Facebook feed when I was pregnant with Matteo.[3] To solidify the message, a friend living in London emailed me the same article. It said that Dutch babies smile, giggle and cuddle up to their parents and loved ones a lot more at the age of six months than their American counterparts. According to the researchers, the temperamental differences could be explained by the different parenting practices.

Nowhere is the divide more evident than in cognitive stimulation. The Dutch do the exact opposite to what most other Western parents are doing. They focus on avoiding overstimulating their babies by sticking to a schedule with specific feeding and sleeping times. But can bringing up a baby who is calm and content really be that simple – a regular routine, plenty of sleep, enough food and the avoidance of overstimulation?

In the Netherlands, there is a huge emphasis on the importance of sleep. In the US and the UK, sleep deprivation is considered a rite of passage: Being able to function on a lack of sleep is something to brag about. Not in the Netherlands. Here, it is taken for granted that babies

The Bugaboo – a Dutch style icon

If there's one thing frugal Dutch parents will spend a lot of money on, it's a quality stroller. And it was a Dutchman who came up with a model that combines ease of use and practicality with good design credentials (and an eye-watering price): the Bugaboo. The chief designer of the Bugaboo, Max Barenburg, designed the first model in 1994 for his graduation project at the Design Academy in Eindhoven. The modular stroller was both sturdy and smart and could be used on urban streets and countryside walks. By 2002, Miranda in *Sex and the City* was seen pushing her newborn through the streets of New York. It became the buggy favored by the stars, with Elton John, Madonna, Gwyneth Paltrow and Catherine Zeta Jones all being photographed pushing one. Even Kate Middleton joined the brigade.

will sleep and allow their parents to sleep as well. And the Dutch are uncompromising about the sanctity of sleep. Recent research declared that the Dutch, on average, get more sleep than anyone else in the world – a total of eight hours and twelve minutes each night.[4]

With a little help from the *consultatiebureau*

In the Netherlands, family, friends, neighbors and acquaintances aren't the only ones to greet the newest member of the family. A day or two after a baby is born a nurse from the local children's health clinic visits the family home, and so begins the regimen of the socially mandated, regular follow-up checkups at the *consultatiebureau* (CB) – the Dutch equivalent of the American well-baby and British well-child clinic visits that take place during the first four years of a baby's life. Every month or so, Matteo's height and weight are monitored, as well as his motor and speech development. It's also where Matteo receives all his vaccinations, free of charge. Any deviation from the average growth and development charts may warrant further investigation by the pediatrician. Because of the CB's notoriously diligent consultation of baby growth charts, some nickname it the Consternation Bureau.

Marlieke, the nurse from the clinic, comes bearing a gift – the Growth Guide, a blue book with a plastic cover that records a child's medical history and serves as an instructional manual for parents. It transpires that there is a universally accepted way of raising babies and children in the Netherlands.

At first I scoffed at the idea of this official Dutch parenting manual. I didn't appreciate being told how to parent my baby, especially when I came from another, quite different culture. It seemed so impersonal. Could there really be a one-size-fits-all method that worked? Did there have to be a manual? How hard could parenting be? Plus, I already had my parenting experts: Gina Ford's *The Contented Little Baby Book*, Elizabeth Pantley's *The No-Cry Sleep Solution*, Harvey Karp's *The Happiest Baby on the Block* and Heidi Murkoff's *What to Expect the First Year*.

Tips from the *consultatiebureau*'s growth guide:[5]

1. Regular daily routine

A baby will cry less if he knows what is going to happen in his day-to-day life. Keeping to the same daily sequence of activities will make him feel at ease: sleeping, waking, feeding (a baby may appear sleepy after being fed, but it is usually just a question of recovery after feeding), cuddling or soothing.

2. Put the baby to bed when she is tired but still awake

If a child is used to falling asleep by herself, she will sleep as much as necessary and will wake refreshed. A child who always needs help to get to sleep will wake up at every unexpected sound, or if she moves in her sleep. It may take a baby from five to twenty minutes, during which time she may whine or cry, to drop off to sleep.

3. Predictable activities

A baby should sleep in a quiet place, such as a cradle, bed, stroller or crib, in the arms of his father or mother or in a sling. However, it is useful for your baby to learn to sleep in his own crib.

4. Prevent too much outside distraction

You can do this by making sure the radio and TV are not switched on all day, not putting a baby aged less than three months under a baby gym for a long time, not placing her in front of the TV and by restricting visitors, who may disturb her sleeping habits.

5. Rest

Make sure your baby has a healthy mix of sleep and being awake and quiet surroundings, and do not take him on more than one outing a day.

> **6. Tuck him in tightly in bed**
>
> A baby often sleeps better when he can't flail his arms and legs
> around. Make up the bed so that the blanket reaches up to the
> baby's shoulders and his feet touch the bottom of the bed. Tuck
> in the blanket snugly, and your child will be really comfortable.

My biggest concern about the Dutch method was that it advocated the cry-it-out method, first proposed by Dr. Richard Ferber in 1985, although it was standard practice in Holland long before that. My Dutch mother-in-law is a dedicated believer in what is now called *ferberizing* – laying the baby down in the crib, closing the door and ignoring their cries throughout the night.

My friend Roos used a more moderate approach that has since been developed. You lay the baby in the crib, wait five minutes, then, if the baby cries, go in to console them verbally, but leave them in the crib. You continue to do this until the baby falls asleep. Roos emphasizes that, of course, with either method, the baby should be well fed and in a clean diaper. Albeit reluctantly, I have to concede that there is something in it. Roos' first baby slept through the night by the age of three months, while I had to wait a year and a half for my first solid, uninterrupted eight hours' sleep after having my first child.

Dutch babies follow a schedule

The Dutch are notoriously organized and value their routine, so it's no surprise that Dutch babies follow a schedule. Like most of my US peers, I fed my firstborn on demand and let him sleep when he wanted to. Doting mom that I was, I would watch Julius for signs that he was hungry or sleepy and allow him to dictate the order of the day, feeding him whenever he seemed to need it, even if it was every hour and all through the night.

"Having a schedule for babies is just common sense," says Yvonne, a Dutch mom whose daughter Noa goes to preschool with Julius. She's come over to meet Matteo, and so that Julius and Noa can play. "I put both of my girls on a schedule recommended by the baby wellness clinic. Initially, it was difficult, but the girls were so much easier to handle if we stuck to a routine. I wanted to be the best mother I could for them. Giving them a regular schedule from the beginning was important. From day one, really."

"But what if babies have an internal rhythm that doesn't match the recommended schedule. What if they're hungry or tired?"

Yvonne continues, cuddling Matteo, who is all smiles, "When Noa's baby sister gets fussy, I simply put her to bed. It usually coincides with the recommended schedule anyway. See it as more of a guide than an unbreakable list of rules. It's just supposed to help you create a consistent routine for your baby."

I follow Yvonne's advice. I want to find out about this famous schedule at Matteo's four-week appointment. My motivation is selfish: I want to start sleeping through the night again myself, as soon as possible. The doctor, a middle-aged man with curly black hair and kind eyes, is a physician after my own heart. He takes the time to get to know all the children and parents who come through the doors of his clinic.

"So, Doctor," I say, "what can I do to put my four-week-old baby on a schedule?" I'm holding my iPhone open at Evernote, perhaps a little enthusiastically, as I cradle Matteo.

The doctor stares back at me, amused. Perhaps my good-ol'-American-go-getter attitude is a bit too much at eight o'clock in the morning. He answers slowly and deliberately, carefully choosing his words and purposely maintaining eye contact with me. "Right now, your goal is to feed Matteo. You have to keep in mind that he was born premature, so he's working really hard to catch up. Let him feed as much as he wants, when he wants. When he's a couple of weeks older, we can talk again."

I nod my head, and he must sense my disappointment. I wonder how much longer I can go on without a good night's sleep. But I am also relieved. This isn't a strict schedule at all: This is feeding on demand, just like I did with Julius. It is the same story at our next three visits. Matteo is measured and weighed and his growth is compared to the Dutch average. I plead to be allowed to start the magic schedule, but the doctor simply tells me to continue what I'm doing.

I carry on following the cues Matteo gives me. By four months old, his daily routine is pretty much predictable. He takes two naps during the day, in the morning for about an hour and in the afternoon for two. In the evening, I put him down by seven, and he sleeps for five hours, waking at midnight for a feeding and again at around 3:00 AM, then sleeping until six. Technically, if one counts sleeping through the night as the ability to sleep for a five-hour stretch, Matteo has done it by himself.[6]

The next time I visit the clinic, I am still keen to get the doctor's recommended schedule. I politely but more assertively confront him. It's not only for me, but for the sake of this book as well. "So now that Matteo's four months old and is obviously growing well, can I *please* put him on your special schedule?" I ask.

The doctor smiles. "You don't need one. Matteo has already decided what his schedule will be."

The sleep experts

While researching the differences between sleeping patterns in babies in the US and the Netherlands, I discover the work of Dr. Sara Harkness and Dr. Charles Super, a husband-and-wife team who teach Human Development, Pediatrics and Public Health at the University of Connecticut. Harkness and Super have been examining parents' cultural beliefs and childcare practices across the world for over thirty years.

As soon as I speak to them on the phone, we start chatting as if I were one of their former students and they my favorite professors.

In 1996, they published their findings in a book called *Parents' Cultural Belief Systems: Their Origins, Expressions and Consequences*. They introduced the idea that every society intuitively believes it knows the right way to raise a child. The parents' cultural beliefs can be observed in their daily family life. These are the everyday choices we make as parents without realizing that we're making them, because they're ingrained in us. These cultural parenting practices, in turn, are likely to influence the way our children behave.[7]

It's no wonder that books like Amy Chua's *Battle Hymn of the Tiger Mother*, Pamela Druckerman's *Bringing Up Bébé* and Harvey Karp's *The Happiest Babies on the Block* are read voraciously. Parents today have been indoctrinated with a belief that how we parent a child determines their future. Harkness and Super found that the Netherlands was the perfect country to analyze when it came to infants and preschoolers. "When compared with Americans, the Dutch emphasized the importance of their infants and toddlers staying calm, relaxed, rested and in a regular routine," observed Harkness. "When the child doesn't have a regular schedule, the baby is fussy. Mothers would say that their child needed regularity. They were very sensitive to that."

Their findings were pivotal to the discovery of an important difference between child-rearing practices in the US and the Netherlands: At six months, Dutch babies slept an average of two hours longer than a comparison sample of American babies—fifteen hours a day in total, compared to thirteen hours.[8] *Two extra hours.* Two precious extra hours of sleep for me. Hallelujah!

And the idea of the parent–infant "sleep struggle," ubiquitous among both Americans and the British, was not an issue for the Dutch.[9] In other words, Dutch parents did not complain of sleep deprivation. This is mind-boggling. There's a billion-dollar industry in the English-speaking world of self-proclaimed parenting experts and sleep gurus trying to help parents desperate for sleep. What is it that the Dutch are doing differently? What is their secret?

"There is a common expression that sums up the Dutch parenting ethnotheory: '*Rust, Regelmaat en Reinheid*' ('rest, regularity and cleanliness'), otherwise known as the Dutch three Rs," says Harkness. The three Rs were "powerfully represented in differences in the amount that babies slept, as well as how they were cared for while awake."

The Dutch three Rs not only make Dutch babies happier, more cuddly and easier to console, they also result in that holy grail for parents: more sleep.

"Here is something interesting for you," Super tells me over the phone. "Keep in mind that the extra two hours of sleep for the Dutch babies was during the day, during the phase of 'quiet sleep.' That, in infants, is what matures into the stages of non-REM sleep for older children and adults. And that is when the human growth hormone is secreted." Super adds, "Of course, there are several factors that influence height. But isn't it interesting that the Dutch also happen to be the tallest people in the world?"

"With everything that you've witnessed, would you two go Dutch yourselves, when it comes to parenting?" I muster the courage to ask.

"Well, all things considered, in general work-life terms, rather than just in parenting, I would rather be American than Dutch," says Harkness.

I'm a bit taken aback. "Why?" I ask.

"I'll explain it through a story I've told thousands of times already. When we were doing our research in the Netherlands, we needed more data to complete our sample. So we asked all our research assistants to interview one additional family. As we went around the table, one by one they refused. None of them felt they had the additional time, even though it seemed that the project might otherwise fail," recalls Dr. Harkness, her voice betraying a hint of the disappointment she felt all those years ago. "That would definitely not have happened in the States. They would all have been worried about losing their jobs! But the more fundamental point for me was that making an extra effort, going the extra mile to achieve a goal, is an American value that I had taken for granted up until that point. To me, that's part of what makes life exciting and satisfying."

I try my best not to laugh. The Dutch take the work-life balance very seriously: They work to live. Most American and British professionals I know, on the other hand, live to work, their unrelenting drive to succeed making them available twenty-four hours a day if needed. Working hard, or at least appearing to, is important to them.

When American and British professional women become mothers, they apply this same focus and level of dedication to parenting. Harkness acknowledged that American mothers are struggling with motherhood. "They've been pushed too far in the direction of intensive parenting, intensive mothering. Quality time and special time taken to the max, where there is not enough time for anything else, including one's own needs. It's just not sustainable, especially if you have more than one child."

Harkness could have been describing me. I was such a sanctimommy with my first child. One step shy of eating my own placenta, I was an attachment-parenting disciple. I would go for days without showering. I don't think I left our apartment regularly until Julius was six months old. He never cried much, because I was so in tune with his every need. Since I didn't let him "cry it out," he was able to feed at any point during the night, and of course I did without sleep. I almost lost my mind, but I thought this was what being a good mother entailed.

"Before I go, I have one more question. Did you witness any 'crying it out' in your research in the Netherlands? Was it common practice? How *did* the Dutch get their babies to sleep through the night?"

"We barely witnessed any crying it out – only in some special cases. What the Dutch did was to stick to a very strict schedule and routine, and their babies fell asleep naturally," Harkness recalls. "And it seems to work. Dutch babies sleep the most out of all the cultures that we've studied."

What could I be doing wrong? Am I not relaxed enough? I thought I was for Matteo, but perhaps he senses my ingrained American anxiety?

Rina discovers more about the Dutch three Rs

It turns out that the three Rs, the Dutch national philosophy of child-rearing, is based on a booklet written by a district nurse in 1905 entitled *Reinheid, rust en regelmaat*. The book's subtitle perfectly summarizes the calm and relaxed Dutch approach to parenting: *A concise explanation of how mothers can care for their infants in the least burdensome way*. This suggests that having a baby is not in itself a burden but rather that parents can make it burdensome.

I seek advice from pediatrician Dr. Mark Hoetjer. I meet him at the hospital in Doorn where he works. "*Reinheid* means 'cleanliness.' But let's be honest, that's not the most important thing. It really isn't necessary to obsess about hygiene and germs like I see some American and German expat parents do. Rest and regularity means that feeding your child should take priority; you shouldn't try to fit it in between other things. I think in the first couple of months, you should fit everything around the most important thing: that is, feeding your child," explains Dr. Hoetjer. "If you feed your child in a hurry, whether you are breastfeeding or formula feeding, it is not good.

"Here is a good example for the idea of 'rest.' If you are working, and you know you have to be at work at 8:00 AM and the baby was up at 5:00 AM with a temperature, then everyone is stressed out, including the baby. But if you decide to take a sick day and go with the flow, then the baby will be much calmer. You can just pick up your child, take her into bed with you and stay relaxed until her temperature goes down. If the mother is stressed, the child will be stressed, and that will make matters worse."

"So: sleep. When am *I* supposed to get some sleep?" I finally ask.

"Everybody is woken up by their baby, including Dutch parents. But the point is to go back to sleep again." Dr. Hoetjer shrugs. "Sometimes you can get an uninterrupted night after three months, but sometimes only after a year, sometimes maybe even two years."

I prod some more. "How do I teach my baby to sleep through the night, or does it happen by itself?"

"It will happen naturally. The moment you try to teach them, things will go wrong because the baby will feel your stress," says Dr. Hoetjer. "For example, if you go to your child and plead, 'Go to sleep, go to sleep. *Please* go to sleep,' it won't work. Sometimes, ignoring and leaving him to cry for a bit can help."

Dr. Hoetjer's advice makes sense to me. With my second baby, I feel a lot more relaxed. Matteo still wakes up once or twice in the middle of the night but, at four months old, it's to be expected. When he does wake up to feed, he usually goes back to sleep right away. I simply don't have the time or the energy to entertain him at all hours of the night, as I did with his brother. And Matteo seems to understand that.

"I read in a research study that new parents in the Netherlands don't suffer the sleep problems that are common among Americans. Is that your experience?" I ask.

"Sometimes we do admit infants into the hospital. If a child doesn't sleep at all through the night for months, then we will investigate. But then, in the hospital, as often as not, the child will fall asleep straight away."

"Really?" I knew I sounded skeptical. This Dutch scenario just sounds a bit too easy and perfect.

"Well, OK, six out of ten times, the baby will go to sleep straight away. Why? Because the mother is not allowed to stay in the room. What happens is that the child will start crying. The nurse will come in and tell the child, 'Listen, I have four other patients.' She may not say it out loud, but the child will feel it. 'There is no negotiation here. I am leaving you. I have other things to do.'"

He pauses and smiles at Matteo, who is busy sucking his thumb.

"I've done some experiments with that myself. It's called the ten-minute method. Some pediatricians and child psychologists recommend it. So if a child starts crying during the night, you go in, but leave the child in bed. You say, 'It's OK. Mommy is here. But you have to go to sleep.' And then you go away. If the child starts crying again, go back in. Do it over and over again until the child is asleep. This way, the child learns that there is no room for negotiation." Dr. Hoetjer is pretty much describing the method Roos used to get her babies to sleep through the night.

Where Rina does Dutch parenting her way

Armed with all the advice I had gathered, I went all out to establish rest and regularity with Matteo. I interpret "regularity" as keeping the pattern of our daily life as regular as possible, and "rest" as ensuring that Matteo sleeps twice during the day and is in bed by seven o'clock every evening. It really does work, and it really is that easy. There's no need to hire an expensive sleep consultant, or pore over dozens of sleeping guidebooks. Though Matteo does sometimes wake up in the middle of the night, mainly due to teething, we're all getting much more sleep.

The other secret? Being relaxed, accepting all the bumps and hiccups that come along the way and keeping an open mind. Like childhood, becoming a mom shouldn't be rushed or overmanaged. There's absolutely no shame in not keeping it all together all the time.

The latest parenting advice in from Denmark is to put babies to sleep outside in the daytime. Some Dutch crèches have even built special insulated outdoor cribs where babies can sleep blissfully in winter.

Initially, I was hesitant about this. Wouldn't he get cold or get sick? What if something happened to him? But I knew that the moment I put Matteo in the stroller for a walk he would fall asleep. One day, I thought that perhaps it would be no different if I just left him out in the garden in the stroller after he fell asleep during our daily walk. And it wasn't. Matteo absolutely loves sleeping in his stroller. He's safely warm in his snow suit and bunting bag. He can sleep outside for two to three hours at a time. Sometimes I even have to wake him up. And it means I can have some precious, undistracted time for myself, without fear of disturbing him.

Michele's experience of the three Rs

When Ben was born, the maternity nurse introduced me to the three Rs. I'd barely held a baby before, so it was lucky she showed me how to bathe him. I was scared I'd drop him and he'd drown, he was so small and vulnerable. She showed me how to change a diaper, too. As far as rest and regularity went, I was advised to put him on a schedule and keep a breastfeeding diary. Of course, as a first-time mom, I was very conscientious about this. I still have it; it shows how the times of his feedings and sleeps gradually shifted as he grew, everything going according to plan. My main problem was that Ben was a very slow feeder and could take an hour to feed from one breast. My mother-in-law told me to tickle his feet to stop him dozing on the breast. The advice from the breastfeeding center was also helpful. The idea is not to let your baby get into the habit of snacking on demand, or using your nipple as a pacifier, but to gradually increase the period between feedings so that his stomach is full each time. Random snacking is discouraged in older children, too. There is a standard routine for schoolchildren of breakfast, a snack at first break time, lunch, and then nothing until an early dinner.

This may explain the lower levels of obesity in the Netherlands – that and all the cycling. We'd been told that Ben would probably start sleeping through the night when he started on solid food, and this turned out to be the case.

The only difficulty we had was getting him to fall asleep in the evenings. I can't remember who suggested it but, after a while, we decided to let him cry it out. I stood outside his door for increasing periods of time (one minute, two, then five), going into his room periodically to reassure him but not picking him up. After four nights, he was falling asleep on his own. My husband was very keen to get the children on a schedule and is still rather strict about it. Dutch people believe that children stay calm and relaxed when they are in a routine. They shouldn't have to fit in around their parents' needs too much.

My second baby, Ina, was a whole new ball game. She'd drain a breast in five minutes flat and slept through the night between the age of six weeks and six months. In typical second-time-parent fashion, I didn't keep a diary for her. However, when she moved on to solids, she stopped sleeping through the night, partly due to reflux. We tried everything to keep her on a schedule, but her body had other ideas. That said, she greatly appreciates routine, so our attempts to regulate her eating and sleeping remained important as she grew older. But I have to confess that, at eight years old, Ina is still not a great sleeper.

4

Joyful Illiterate Preschoolers

*In which Rina accepts that you don't have to
push toddlers to learn to read*

Imagine if you will a scene in a video where there's one dark-haired three-year-old child surrounded by blond children. He seems a bit lost. He's in a colorful classroom with shelves and boxes overflowing with books, art supplies, building blocks, playdough, Duplo, toys, dollhouses and a play corner complete with a kitchen, a shop and a rack of dress-up clothes.

He's in the middle of the room, along with the other children. Everyone else seems to be intently following the nursery teacher, mimicking her hand gestures as music is played. But not him. He has other plans, or he's bored by what the teacher is doing. He decides to roll around on the floor instead, paying no attention to her. Another child also keeps himself apart, his face pressed against the glass door. This child seems to be more interested in the leafy playground with its red jungle gym, sandbox and playhouses. The teacher continues doing what she's doing and just lets the two boys be.

The video shows Julius at his *peuterspeelzaal* (playschool). Julius attends playschool four times a week: twice in the morning and twice in the afternoon on different days, each session lasting approximately three and a half hours. At each session there are, at most, sixteen children, supervised by two nursery teachers. Julius happens to be a boy of very few words. He is quite shy and doesn't talk much around strangers or in big groups, so he is getting extra help to develop his Dutch-language skills – but still through play rather than any formal instruction. It's a fabulous, convenient setup; a safe space where Julius can explore and develop his social skills for a few hours while I enjoy the opportunity to give baby Matteo some one-on-one attention.

A typical session at playschool involves a standard pattern: First, at drop-off, parents are encouraged to stay and read or do a puzzle with their child before saying goodbye. This is followed by circle time, when the children and teachers greet each other and the day's arts and crafts activity is introduced; then there's time for child-initiated free play and the arts and crafts activity; followed by a second circle time to listen to music or do some other activity; and, finally, free play again until pick-up time. There's no attempt to teach the letters of the alphabet or numbers. What playschool is all about – true to its name – is play. It revolves around children doing what they enjoy best – playing, and interacting with other children.

As I watch the video, I'm not sure how I feel. I waver between wanting to laugh and cry at watching my son being allowed to simply be himself, without being pushed to participate or pay attention. The cool, calm Dutch mom I'm trying to embody loves the laid-back approach. Yet I can't silence this nagging voice in my head: *Is it enough?*

"I wonder if we're doing the right thing," I confide to Bram later that evening after watching the video again with him. We are lying in bed – my preferred time for heart-to-heart conversations and his preferred time to zone out and read. "I'm not sure whether sending Julius to this preschool is good for him. He's not learning anything – not the alphabet or his numbers. Do you think he's falling behind?"

If there's one thing I learned from my immigrant parents, it is that education is everything. Excelling at school is the only way to a better life, or so the mantra goes. It's about survival. Starting as early as you can translates into learning more; the early bird catches the worm. My Facebook feed is littered with my proud friends back home demonstrating their children's accomplishments: videos of four-month-olds in Bumbo chairs entranced by *Sesame Street*, eight-month-olds completing puzzles, one-year-olds playing educational games on iPads. All of this is meant to give a child a head start to ensure future success.

In true tiger-mom-to-be fashion, I prepared for my son's education before he was even born. I read books such as *Brain Rules for Baby* by John Medina, bought over a hundred books to make sure that we started reading from the moment he was born, and insisted on only wooden toys with nontoxic paint. And yet, here I am, almost four years later, with a child who has yet to get a grasp on speaking, let alone get ahead with reading, writing and arithmetic.

"Don't worry so much," Bram assures me. "I turned out normal enough, didn't I? I wasn't messed up too badly by the Dutch system." He's right, of course. Without much early help from either his schools or his parents, my husband still managed to get an education and a master's degree.

In the US and the UK, parents, with all the best intentions, and tuning in to current unspoken cultural expectations, are pushing their children to learn at younger and younger ages. The pressure on British and American kindergartens and preschools is to function more like elementary schools. A study titled "Is Kindergarten the New First Grade?" compares kindergarten classrooms in the US in 1998 and in 2010, and concludes that later kindergarten teachers have higher academic expectations for their pupils and dedicate more time to the formal teaching of reading and arithmetic.[1] Sadly, this means there is less time for art, music and child-initiated play. In the Netherlands and in Scandinavia, this is not the case.

A Dutch friend of mine, Maria, who is a children's book writer and illustrator living in the San Francisco Bay Area with her husband and six-year-old son, muses, "Being an outsider, I'm constantly amazed at how American moms are different from Dutch moms. My mind is blown on a daily basis. There's this preoccupation with reading at a young age – they believe that the ability for younger kids to learn to read and write and recognize numbers will somehow mean more success later in their academic life.

"I read somewhere that one of the main differences is that, in Europe, parents' main concern is for their children to be happy and find a community that they feel at home in. The main concern of American parents is for their kids to become successful in life," says Maria. "If you're primarily concerned with your child's success, you'll want your kid to go to the best possible school.

"There is a lot of fear. There is also a lot of guilt. I can't afford a great private preschool, but I don't worry about that. If you give your kid love and see to it that they are happy, they are going to be fine. I am really grateful that I grew up in Holland and that I have that outsider perspective. It does keep me a lot more grounded about being a parent. It doesn't let me get caught up in that whole competitive thing."

Another Dutch mom living in San Francisco is Ottilie. She says, "I have close contact with my cousins, who have kids the same age back home, so we have talked about this a lot. My findings are that, initially, the kids in San Francisco are ahead in reading and even math, because they start them on it so early. But by second grade I see their head start stall, as the teachers are still working on trying to bring all kids up to the same level. My view is that this is because not all kids are ready to learn to read and write so early. In Holland, they start later and more slowly, but by second grade they are all reading and counting, and can advance together. Their brains have had more time to develop naturally because they have had more unstructured playtime in their early years, when that is so important. I felt sorry for my son to have to sit still and concentrate from such an early age for such long hours.

"Both my kids started reading 'late' – when they were almost seven. The school flagged them for reading help at the age of six, but I turned it down. I wanted to wait, since it's normal that not all kids are ready to read at five or six," says Ottilie. "And then, when they were turning seven, they both started reading. They advanced super fast and have since been avid readers, reading at higher levels than is standard for their grade. If they had had specialist help, that program would have received the credit for this. But I'm convinced that kids, as long as they don't have dyslexia or other learning issues, will simply learn how to read when they are ready."

I couldn't help but be impressed. Ottilie managed to hold her ground: She was able to keep her pragmatic wits about her even in the overachieving atmosphere of San Francisco.

Where a Dutch mom spells it out for Rina

Curious to know more about Dutch parenting, and dying to make a new mommy friend, I invite Jet, whose two-year-old, Jaime, goes to playschool with Julius, for a mommy date. She and her family have just recently returned to the Netherlands after spending eleven years abroad as expats. We meet at the HEMA, a popular Dutch store where you can find almost anything, including a full breakfast at a bargain price. For just two euros, we buy an omelet sandwich, a croissant with jam, a glass of orange juice and a coffee.

"Why would a child of our sons' age need to learn their ABCs? Why can't you just let them play?" Jet asks. "Playing with other kids is just as important, if not more. If you encourage that in an early stage, it will help your child in the future.

"Primary school can be quite a harsh world. For example, some kids will throw birthday parties and not invite everyone in the class. And some moms cry over this because their child isn't popular with the other kids yet. The playschools understand the importance of developing their kids' social skills at an early age – how to make friends, take turns, be nice, and how to play with each other."

"But what about actual learning?" I ask.

"What do you mean? Have you ever sat down at the playschool and watched what they actually do? You know that every morning they sit in a circle? When I was there, they were learning about the weather. The teacher will ask, 'Jaime, can you tell me what the weather is like today?' and point to a chart that has three different pictures on it: a sun with blue skies, a rain cloud with water droplets, and a cloud with swirls to represent a windy day. She'll then tell Jaime to get up and look out of the window, and then pick a picture. Jaime goes to the window, looks up at the blue sky and points at the right picture. That, to me, is learning."

I want my child to be normal – Michele's story

I've never really believed that it was good to squeeze every last drop of potential out of a child as soon as possible. What's the rush? American and British parents can get quite competitive, comparing the milestones their babies and toddlers have reached. Here in Holland, very little attention is paid to whether a young child can read or write at an early age. In fact, there is a kind of veto on talking about it. A Dutch girlfriend alerted me to something expats might overlook: the tendency to downplay achievements here. There is a social pressure to be as average as possible and to never show off. This explains the lack of mompetition, and why no one is keen to point out their children's talents.

When Ina was three she was a clingy, shy child, but she could write a few words she'd taught herself: "Mama," "Papa," "Ina," "Ben." She'd write them on everything. At her age-three checkup at the children's health clinic, she wandered into the appointment clutching a postcard on which she'd written her words while amusing herself in the waiting room. But the nurse simply ignored that and got on with measuring her growth before asking her to stack up three blocks.

I have helped Ina when she has wanted it, but I have never pushed her to learn. When she started school just before her fourth birthday, her teacher noticed her keenness to learn and gave her worksheets so she could practice the alphabet and do some math problems. She developed a love of math around that age and would lie in bed reciting her times tables. When she continued to learn faster than the other children in her class, she was moved up to the third grade, which is more focused on learning. The school's approach is generally to provide gifted children with extra material to deepen and broaden their knowledge, rather than automatically push them up the next step on the ladder. When Ina grew bored despite this, she was put up another grade. For us, however, for other Dutch parents and her teachers, social skills are much more important than academic achievements. I want her to be happy with her friends, not some intensively educated, precocious child. With the teachers at school, we are currently considering keeping her in the top class of primary school for an extra year so that she doesn't go to secondary school at the age of ten.

In which Rina embraces playschool ideology

Eager to reduce my anxiety about Julius' learning once and for all, I decided to speak to his teachers before the start of playschool one morning. Anna, Dingena and Irma are all women in their sixties, approachable and kind grandmotherly types who clearly enjoy being around toddlers. They are also adept at multitasking; they answer my questions while preparing for the day's art activity.

Apparently, I'm not the only parent concerned about the lack of formal teaching. The modern mood of intensive educating has reached even our neck of the woods. Other parents have voiced their concerns about their child not starting to read and their worries about the possibility of them falling behind in elementary school. But the playschool teachers are constantly trying to reassure parents that play, rather than formal instruction, is best.

With their combined eighty years of teaching experience, the teachers remain committed to the active and exploratory early-childhood pedagogy and are well used to reassuring worried parents like me.

"What's most important for us is that we offer opportunities here for a child to develop on his own, at his own pace," explains Anna. "That means providing a wide variety of many different types of play materials, both inside the classroom and outside in the playground, for them to choose from. And we do lots and lots of talking with them, encouraging them to explore and following their lead in conversation."

Judging by the controlled chaos of tempting toys, books and arts and crafts materials, they certainly offer a good choice for a child to develop his curiosity and get lost in his imagination. Even I have a hard time resisting riffling through one of the toy-filled boxes. I also see that, with two teachers and the small class size, there's ample room for them to have one-on-one conversations with the kids and really get to know each child for the two years they're under their care.

"We want them to learn how to socialize with their peers. We encourage them to play with each other so they can learn social skills – how to share, be patient, be confident," says Irma. "And then we also do group activities, like reading a story together, singing songs and making something as a class."

"When parents come here and voice their concern about their child not being challenged enough," says Dingena, "we tell them it's great that their child can recite their ABCs, count up to a hundred and name all the colors, but all it means is that they've demonstrated that they can be monkeys performing a trick. That's all it is. A trick. Not real learning."

It doesn't matter how long I've been in the Netherlands, the blunt way the Dutch put things sometimes makes me feel like I just took a cold shower. "Refreshing" would be an understatement. I had to remind myself that Dingena wasn't necessarily calling my three-year-old a performing monkey. She was just emphasizing the idea that teaching a child to play is far more important than teaching them their alphabet and numbers.

"Yesterday, a child was crying in class – her mama and papa had just had a new baby. So we spent time getting her to explain all the new emotions that she was feeling. That is what we're here for. We teach children how to express their feelings clearly and help them to identify them," adds Anna. "It's not all about learning. It's about developing as a person, learning to speak their own mind and how to get along with other children." If there is one thing the Dutch are good at, it is talking to their children. As soon as they can babble, they encourage them to talk back. It helps to explain why their children are so articulate and confident.

As I cycled home, I wondered whether we really need to be entertaining, training, teaching and pushing our kids all the time, if, without all that, Dutch children turn out so well.

5
Stress-Free Schooling

In which Michele rethinks education

Of all the parenting decisions we have to make, choosing a school seems one of the most fundamental. At the time, nothing seems more important in life than your child's education. My friends back home in London tell me it is an obsession that dominates dinner party conversations, since nobody is ever sure they've made the right decision, whether they've opted for private or state schooling. For the British and for Americans, education is seen as the route to success. The better you do in school, the further you'll go in life. If you don't get your kid into a good nursery school, you won't get them into a good primary school. And a good primary school – or, if you can afford it, a good prep school – is thought to be essential for your son or daughter to get into a decent secondary school in the UK or high school in the US. And, of course, a decent secondary or high school is essential to get good grades and a place at the best university. And in the US, top grades = top universities, or top athlete = full scholarship at top university/lucrative professional sports contract. Many parents will go to any length to get their child into the right school – they will take out an extra mortgage, or move houses, perhaps even to a different town to get into the catchment area for the "right" school.

In the Netherlands, however, it isn't all about getting straight As and getting into the right university. Education here has a different purpose. It is traditionally seen as the route to a child's well-being and their development as an individual. There are two kinds of Dutch higher education qualifications: research-orientated degrees offered by universities and profession-orientated degrees offered by colleges. You don't need specific grades to gain admission to most college programs: All you need is to pass your high school exams at the right level – this is enough to guarantee a place. What's more, students don't have to compete for places. So in order to come to grips with the Dutch school system, I had to unpack a whole lot of psychological baggage and unconscious values and rethink what education was all about. I had to let go of a lot of things I'd been brought up to believe in.

When Ben was two and a half and I was heavily pregnant with Ina, we moved from a small apartment in the south of the city to a house in Amsterdam Noord. Noord, which means "north," is sometimes fondly and sometimes not so fondly referred to as "Siberia," probably because of its Arctic winds. It was an area my husband, a born-and-bred Amsterdammer, had only ventured into once before and was rather terrified of. It is separated from the rest of the city by the cold channel of the river IJ and rarely features on tourist maps. Noord is where the gallows used to stand and has been long associated in the popular imagination with criminals, poverty and experimental housing projects where the government dumps "antisocial elements."

Back in 2007, it brought to mind high-rise tower blocks, a large immigrant population and a stunningly ugly, white-plastic-clad shopping center.

Still, I'd moved to Amsterdam from scruffy Harlesden in northwest London, which was full of Caribbean fried-chicken joints, Afro hairdressers and Portuguese cafés, so I was looking forward to the area's diversity. Amsterdam Noord felt like a home away from home. I found a spacious old house that was cheap and bordered a park. And off we went, typical harbingers of gentrification, along with a whole host of other new arrivals, about to turn Amsterdam Noord into the Dutch equivalent of New York's Williamsburg or London's Hoxton.

My husband was left with the job of finding a primary school for Ben. He would need to register him before his third birthday. With only state schools to consider, we soon had a list of options. Right from the start, I'd been thrilled by the idea that, in the Netherlands, parents didn't have the stress of having to decide whether to send their children to a private school. I'd been educated at a provincial grammar school and the difference between my education and that of the privately educated kids was very apparent to me in my first year of university, where I had to play catch-up. Later in life, employed in the privileged bastion of publishing, I'd frequently sidestepped the question of which school I'd been to, painfully aware that this was crucial to your social standing and people's perceptions of you. You were one of *us* or you were one of *them*.

In our new neighborhood, there was an array of options open to us. First of all, there were several "concept schools," each based on a particular progressive teaching method. Historically, these have all been foreign imports, like the Montessori system from Italy, the Dalton Plan from America or the German child-based learning program the Jena Plan. There were also more traditional schools: religious – Christian or Muslim – and nondenominational, secular state schools. None of the options cost money.

We visited a few of the schools, and I was immediately struck by the calm and cheerful atmosphere in our local Montessori. The building wasn't anything special – a single-story 1980s snake of classrooms, walls painted white and yellow. Colorful children's art hung everywhere. The corridors featured play areas with sandboxes, doll's houses and tables for creative projects and were dotted with happy-looking children. The classrooms were quiet and filled with children working away not just with books but also with beads, wooden blocks and cards. The youngest were often seated on mats on the floor, involved in educational games. All the children looked cheerful and relaxed. In the US and the UK, Montessori schools are part of the private system. Here they are available to all. I counted my blessings.

Amsterdam has twenty-eight Montessori schools. The first one was founded in 1914, and by the 1920s they had become popular. Anne Frank attended a Montessori primary school before she went into hiding. Looking at the philosophy, it's easy to see why it appeals to the Dutch. Like the Dalton and Jena Plan schools, which are also popular here, the emphasis is on independence and helping others. The basic premise is "help me to do it myself."

Maria Montessori believed that adults – parents and teachers – shouldn't impose ideas on children, and that natural self-development is preferable. Instead of all the children learning the same things together at the same time, they choose to learn at their own pace, on an individual basis. Montessori thought that children should be encouraged to surf their own wave of interest in a particular topic, or skill, and that you shouldn't force learning on them. In fact, this attitude has permeated into the wider education system in the Netherlands. In all Dutch primary schools, kids start school at four but don't officially start structured learning – reading, writing and arithmetic – until they are six years old, in Year 3. If they do show interest in these subjects earlier, they are provided with the materials to explore them for themselves. Both of my children learned to read and write in their first year of school this way, but there was no pressure. Friends who learned to read later, in the third year, at six or seven, showed no particular disadvantage in having learned later and soon caught up.

According to the American National Institute for Child Health and Human Development, "Reading is the single most important skill necessary for a happy, productive and successful life. A child that is an excellent reader is a confident child and has a high level of self-esteem."[1] By not forcing children to read too early, reading becomes a pleasure, not a chore.

The importance of social skills

We had picked our Montessori school because it made such a good impression on us, not because we knew much about its methods. Looking back now, I guess I had already become quite Dutch. I know a lot of British or American parents would have researched the schools available, compared charts of results, interviewed the teachers, and so on. That simply didn't occur to me, perhaps because I was following my husband's lead. But the first time my son came home with a school report, aged four, I confess to being shocked. There were no grades, no marks out of ten, no As, Bs or Cs. It did not say that he was top of the class, which his high-achieving mother had been secretly hoping for, and neither did it say he was the bottom. In fact, there was *no* indication of where he stood in comparison to the rest of his class. Instead, the report card featured a row of five dots per category, representing Ben's development:

- Far behind general learning pathway
- Behind general learning pathway
- Follows general learning pathway
- Ahead of general learning pathway
- Far ahead of general learning pathway

These were the only – rather boring and unglamorous – pegs onto which I could project my sad need for affirmation by proxy. It was nothing like the primary school reports I used to have, complete with marks out of twenty and my position in the class.

From the chart, I gleaned that Ben was considered ahead of average, but there was no implication that this was better than being behind. What's more, much of the report focused on his social skills and character, not on academic achievements. I was confronted with my own unchallenged set of values. Why shouldn't social skills be more important than being clever?

The same report format has been used throughout my children's time at primary school: five dots. No marks out of ten, no As, Bs or Cs. Each dot gives me a general idea of how they are doing with particular skills, be it working with others, being organized, or dealing with setbacks. Many other types of schools use this system, too – it's not just Montessori – though some of the more traditional Dutch schools do give graded reports.

The various assessment categories speak volumes. There's General Behavior: The ideal child is independent, calm, modest, self-confident, spontaneous and responsible. There is Care of the Environment, which takes into consideration whether their work is neat and their desk clean and tidy. Relationship with the Teacher is another category: The ideal pupil is helpful, curious, polite, attentive and open to being corrected when wrong. Running parallel to this is Relationship with Other Children: Kids are encouraged to be cooperative, considerate towards others, resilient and good at listening. Finally, the category Attitude to Work assesses the following attributes: standards, level of perseverance, concentration, ability to work independently, listening during lessons, motivation and how quickly your child works.

This is a much more detailed character assessment than I ever had as a child. It's also clear what the key values are and what the school hopes to achieve: not necessarily academic brilliance and high scores but to nurture a child who socializes well and keeps their desk tidy. It seems miles away from the experiences of friends in the UK, where seemingly constant tests appear to be more about reaping good school performance data, raising the school's profile and thus enhancing their ability to get funding, than about the kids taking them.

I ask Anja, one of the Dutch mothers in my book club, what she thinks is important in education. "The main thing is lots of play!" she says. "I'd like my boys to learn to think creatively, but also to be socially adept . . . Apart from that, I think musical development is important."

If you opt for a Montessori, Dalton or Jena Plan school, there is no homework. If you opt for any other type of primary school, there is very little. Most schoolchildren don't get any homework until they leave primary school. Reading around the subject, I come across a growing body of research that suggests that homework for young children is a waste of time and has little or no benefit in enhancing learning or performance.[2] It's a major difference between the Netherlands and the US and UK. Play and having fun are considered more important here than getting ahead academically.

My stepsister, who lives in a small town in Britain, told me that her daughters' primary school asked parents to sign a contract. She had to pledge that she would read with her daughters every night and also do spelling and homework with them. "They even run parent classes explaining how they teach math these days, so you can help them," she added. Like most parents, she works full-time and also has to ferry her girls around to their extracurricular activities. Finding the time to sit down and tutor them through their nightly homework adds a lot of pressure to an already tight daily schedule.

In the UK, the emphasis of the school curriculum remains on academic achievement. I talk to Roman Krznaric, an Oxford-based philosopher whose book *How to Find Fulfilling Work* was a major factor in my own decision to go freelance a couple of years ago. His main field is empathy. "In recent years, the UK government has made the fatal mistake of cutting back on social and emotional learning programs and replacing them with a traditionalist focus on reading, writing and arithmetic," he tells me.

I ask Roman what he thinks British schools could do better. "One of the key things to fall by the wayside is the teaching of empathy skills, which are so important to children's emotional development and ability to relate to others," he explains. "Evidence from school education programs such as Roots of Empathy, which began in Canada and has now reached over three quarters of a million children worldwide, not only shows that empathy can be taught but also that it improves cooperation, reduces bullying and even increases general academic achievement."

Despite Britain's traditionalist focus on reading, writing and arithmetic, a new report from the OECD rated English teenagers aged between sixteen and nineteen at the bottom of the tables of thirty-four developed nations in literacy, and last but one in numeracy. In the same OECD study, the Netherlands came in the top three, along with Finland and Japan. The *Times* reported: "Young people in England are the most illiterate in the developed world and are floundering in math, according to a global report."[3] The Dutch newspapers gleefully wrote that this sounded like "an absurdist joke," reporting that "Dutch people learning English at school know more about the language."[4]

Clear rules are essential

To get a more intimate knowledge of the values of the school my children attend, I talk to the headmistress. I'm sure that her air of friendly authority has informed the pleasant atmosphere in the school. She is a small, sturdy woman who rolls with a gait like a seaman just come ashore, and is due to retire next year. I see her virtually every morning, standing at the door, shaking the hand of every child who comes through. She always insists that it has to be the right hand and that gloves are removed: This is the proper way. Stand in line, walk don't run. If she isn't there to do this, one of the other teachers mans the receiving line.

In her small, spartan office, I explain what this book is going to be about. The first thing she volunteers without any prompting is that she feels it is "absolutely *crucial* that children are happy at school."

I'm surprised. I hadn't expected her to be so forthright about it. I ask how she maintains the peaceful atmosphere in the school. She pauses for a moment. "With clear rules. Rules are essential. When I arrived seventeen years ago, it was chaos. The children would storm into the school like wild animals."

I nod. I can hardly imagine that now.

"Personally greeting them by name at the door means the day starts and stays calm. That brief moment of contact is very important."

It's true: She knows the name of each of the five hundred or so students. When you enter the school, the focus is on the child and their burgeoning independence. Parents are not allowed to help their kids with coats and shoes, even in the first year, and children are expected to carry their own bags. (This leads to lengthy changing sessions before and after PE, even if there's no time left in the middle for gym!)

"When I was a child in England, school was more about academic performance than happiness," I say. "Isn't there pressure to produce as many top grades as possible?"

"Oh, I know, I've visited English schools myself," she replies. "Here, it is about what each child can achieve as an individual. Each child should be making progress based on whatever level they start from, not on standard levels for their age." The headmistress does her best to keep slow learners in the school, feeling that they are better off here than in special schools.

The school has just set up a student council made up of six kids between the ages of nine and twelve, following advice from the inspectorate, a Dutch official who surveys the national state of education yearly. "I was interested to hear what the kids had to say about the school's strengths. I asked them why would they recommend this school to people new to the neighborhood? Do you know what they said? 'The teachers treat you with respect'; 'There's very little bullying'; 'You can learn an awful lot here'; and 'The teachers are nice, but strict in a good way.'

"That's the point," the headmistress continues: "*In a good way*. It's important that there's mutual respect. And there were other positive things." She runs through a mental list of quotes: "'The teachers leave you alone'; 'You can work independently'; 'You don't have to ask for things'; 'And there are lots of parties!'"

It's true that there are often parties and special fun days. The new student council has requested a pajama day, which brings the headmistress to the story of a sleepover she organized in a previous school. "The kids brought their sleeping bags and inflatable mattresses and slept in the gym. I brought my dog, to make us feel safe. We watched a football match, and one of the fathers, who owned a snack bar, came along with *frikandel*[5] and chips."

From the age of six, one-night-away school outings are introduced. This is often the first time the children have been away from home without their parents. They are not allowed to take mobile phones and there is no contact with their parents during these trips, which increase in length as the children grow older. While they are away, they visit a museum or place of interest but are also given lots of time to play outside.

We meet the Happiness Professor

The Netherlands has its very own Professor of Happiness, Ruut Veenhoven of Erasmus University in Rotterdam. A front-runner in happiness research, he has spent many years building and curating a World Database of Happiness, which is freely accessible online.[6] He agreed to talk to Rina and me about his findings, and we met up in an ethnic greasy spoon in Utrecht, close to where he was looking after his grandchildren on what he tells us is a regular "*opa* (grandfather) day."

Professor Veenhoven, a kindly looking man, began our conversation by defining happiness as "life satisfaction": how much an individual enjoys their life as a whole. He warned that many of the tests measure welfare rather than well-being. Moving on, he then mentioned the egalitarian culture in the Netherlands. "We were a seafaring nation, and it was hard to keep control of sailors, so we ended up being less feudal than other countries. This egalitarianism is reflected in our home life, too – there's more equality between child and parent."

He said that Dutch schools provide a "child-friendly education." Children *like* going to school, and this is something that is also reflected in the research UNICEF collated in 2013. Dutch children are among the least likely to feel pressured by schoolwork and scored highly in terms of finding their classmates friendly and helpful.

"Schools here invest more energy in motivation than in achievement," Veenhoven explained. "Achievement is what French and English schools typically focus on," he added. "Actually, our research has shown that social skills are instrumental to happiness. They are much more important than a person's IQ."

We ask if he can tell us more about the relationship between happiness and education, and he leans over the table toward us. "Comparing countries, we found a positive relationship between average education and average happiness. We live happier in modern societies which require an educated population. Yet within modern nations, there is little relation between individual education and happiness. Since there are evident advantages to higher education, there must be counterbalancing disadvantages. We don't yet know where these 'happiness leaks' are, but you certainly don't need to push your child hard for academic achievement for the sake of their later happiness."

After our extensive talk, he then looks at his watch and excuses himself. "It's time I was getting back to my grandchildren. They'll be needing their lunch soon."

The secondary school stream

A few weeks after my pleasant Sunday at the allotment with Ben and Floris, I'm doing an editing job in an office on the Keizersgracht. My cell rings and Ben's name flashes up on the screen.

"Hi, darling. Are you all right?"

"I got the Cito results, Mummy," he says, all in a rush. "I got 545!"

The Cito is a Dutch entrance exam to secondary school (high school). We weren't expecting the results of his test for another four days but, somehow, the school has gotten them to the students earlier. The tests are only intended as confirmation of the school's judgment of which type of secondary education would suit each child best, in terms of both academic ability and temperament. The pragmatic thinking behind this is that a teacher is a better judge of a child than a test. If a student gains a higher Cito score than on previous tests, the school will discuss their recommendation with the child's parents. This won't necessarily result in a change of school choice, but it could. In our case, the test results confirmed the school's impression of Ben, a child who would be able to keep up at grammar school and be happy there. He had already enrolled, so now it was a matter of waiting to see whether he got a place.

Children with the highest average scores and a solid work ethic enter the highest academic school stream – the VWO, from ages twelve to eighteen, which prepares them for university entry. Here they work toward a VWO diploma, which is like a high school diploma with several Advanced Placement (AP) credits, or an International Baccalaureate diploma. It takes six years. The next level of secondary school is HAVO. It offers a general secondary education that equips children for a professional-orientated higher education. Typically, this might be in business, nursing or teaching, but it might also be a foundation course that leads to an academic university education. Lower Cito scores will result in a recommendation for one of the four VMBO – prevocational – streams. These prepare children for vocational or technical training in one of four areas: economy, technology, health care or agriculture, from the age of sixteen on. Sixty percent of all children enter this stream, and I am not aware of any social stigma attached to it. The system also allows for students to move across streams. Ben's total score is just within the band for the more academic VWO stream (545–550) but, in any case, these days, a child's assessment is based on the combined results of the casually presented, biannual tests children take in their last three years at school without any special studying beforehand, plus the teacher's estimation of their abilities and attitude to work.

When I tell friends in the UK about the Dutch school system, their initial reaction is to worry that children will be categorized too early and that this may limit a child's options. But talking to locals, such as the builders working on the wet rot in our foundation over the summer, I find otherwise. One of them has a daughter about to enter her second year in a vocational school (plant and animal science, and agriculture). He is more than happy with the level of her education, and his daughter has already moved up one stream after a year. He feels there is plenty of potential to move up through the streams if the child is capable of it. His daughter is planning to be a horse trainer, helps out at the local stables and is getting an education tailored to her needs. The joiner's daughter, who is twelve and a bookworm, got a place at a local *gymnasium* (academic school) to study VWO and he's pleased she'll have this opportunity.

Ben's tall friend Floris has been recommended for the HAVO stream. He is a quiet, bright boy who has difficulty concentrating. He dives into a book whenever he feels overwhelmed and so doesn't always finish his schoolwork. To my surprise, the teacher has allowed him to sit and read on his own in class, realizing that this means of escape is important to his mental state, and hasn't tried to force him to work harder. Both the school and his parents feel he's probably a late bloomer who will come into his own. Floris himself says he'll work his way up from HAVO to VWO – university-entry level – which is possible in the schools that offer various types of education under one roof. Alternatively, an ambitious HAVO student can do a foundation year at university before joining the VWO kids a year later to get a bachelor's degree. It's something my seventeen-year-old nephew is planning to do, having been held back by a visual handicap that slows his reading.

As in Floris' case, the teachers at our Montessori school err on the side of caution when recommending school streams. I can imagine that if the system were transposed to the UK, there would be parental pressure on the school to be as optimistic as possible. When I'd asked Ben's teacher, Cinthya, whether Ben's better-than-average year (half of the children in his class had VWO recommendations) wouldn't make it difficult for the school next year, she was quite taken aback. "Once expectations have been raised . . . ?" I clarified. She frowned. "Of course not. We just want the children to go to the schools that are right for them." This attitude is so unlike the aspirational anguish in British and American schools, it continues to amaze me every time I'm confronted with it.

"A six is enough"

The noncompetitive Dutch approach to primary school education is interesting; there is no top of the class to aspire to. The same is true of secondary schools, where, once you are in a particular stream, you need only score an average of six out of ten – a passing grade – to stay at this level. I should make it clear that the grading system in the Netherlands doesn't equate to the British or American systems, which are based on percentages. Marks are deducted for mistakes, and perfection (ten out of ten) is virtually unattainable. The bulk of students score sixes and sevens, and this is sufficient to secure their final diplomas. The mean score at high school graduation is 6.4. Only a small percentage of students make an eight average, and this is considered extremely high.[7] It's also important to note that Dutch scores are graded on a curve, so an individual score is also relative to what everyone else scored.

In the academic stream (VWO), if students have made it through with a passing grade, they are considered bright enough to merit a place at a university. There is certainly no grade inflation, which is a big issue in the US and the UK. As a consequence, there is no escalation in competitiveness as students aim for the highest grades to ensure a place at a university. It seems like a very fair system and avoids elitism.

In his recent study of Dutch identity, *Moet kunnen* (Must be possible), cultural historian Herman Pleij explained educational policy in the Netherlands. It concentrates, he writes, on the widest possible section of ability in the middle, rather than on the highest achievers:

> The [concept of the] "golden mean" reverberates through all levels of the education system in the form of the central objective of delivering a maximum number of pupils and students with a qualification. For this, a pass grade is enough. If you want to do better than that, it's entirely up to you.[8]

Aristotle's concept of the "golden mean" – the healthy median, which avoids the vices of the two extremes – is central to Dutch thinking. The common expression we explained earlier – *Doe maar gewoon dan doe je al gek genoeg* (Just act normal, that's crazy enough) – can be applied here, too.

Although there isn't a strongly competitive climate at school, the Dutch do seem to meet with extraordinary success in ideas-driven, creative and entrepreneurial enterprises: Witness the famous Dutch artists, designers and architects, not to mention the twenty-one Nobel Prize winners the country has produced. Also impressive is the list of Dutch inventions (it includes the DVD, the CD, Bluetooth and Wi-Fi). Yet the Dutch educational approach is currently subject to some internal criticism: In the Netherlands there is a new drive toward pushing the highest achievers. Pleij speaks out against this. He believes that moderateness and being average are necessary features of the Dutch system, since they are inclusive and involve the greatest number of students. To take this away and focus on the brilliance of a few will, he believes, reduce the general level of innovation and the country's prosperity and well-being.[9]

The advantage of the Dutch school system at present is that it actively keeps children in the race for as long as possible, as opposed to their being eliminated along the way in a competitive battle to the top.

———

I decide to talk to Arwen, one of my oldest Dutch friends, and her mother about schools. Arwen is around the same age as me. I got to know her when her eldest son and my son became best friends at the crèche. She's a statuesque blond married to a handsome former Olympic athlete, who is also big and blond. They have two gorgeous, sporty boys. She brings her mother round to my house for tea and petits fours one summer's afternoon.

Paulien, Arwen's mom, an elegant seventy-year-old who used to work in the education sector as a special needs advisor, tells me she felt it wasn't at all important what type of school her three children went to. More important to her was the kind of training they would get afterward. "The kind of person you are is what counts. What are your interests? What was your Saturday job as a teenager? If you want to go to university, you need a VWO qualification, but whether you passed with a six or a ten out of ten is irrelevant."

In any case, each of her three children ended up doing something quite different from what they were trained for. One daughter studied law and now makes films for children; another did South American studies and now works at a department store. Arwen trained as a nurse and is now a freelance writer. To their mother, this is proof that, in the end, your school career doesn't really matter.

I ask Arwen whether she has any ambitions for her two sons. "Well, if my children do sports, I want them to get into a good team. And, as for school, you can say it doesn't matter as long as they're happy, which is partly true, but I'm also a *little* bit ambitious for them."

But I don't think she really belongs to that small pocket of pushy parents generally confined to affluent Amsterdam Zuid and the Gooi (the area around Hilversum, the closest the Dutch have to the Hollywood Hills), and she confirms this: "If either of my sons didn't get into the academic stream, it certainly wouldn't keep me awake at night!"

The problem with competition

In my own life, I found the transition from the competitive atmosphere of school and university (where I was always striving to be top of the class) to working life, without its exams and comparative measures, quite difficult. A rat race childhood can set you up for a pervasive sense of disappointment in later life. When the grading stops, so does the source of your self-esteem. In some cases, this may lead you to measure your worth in financial terms, or in sales figures, or by investing your time in sourcing the very best of everything for your child. I don't want this kind of competition-driven stress to be instilled in my own children. I would much rather they learned to value their own achievements rather than needing constant praise or any confirmation that they are better than others.

In an article in *Psychology Today*, Professor Peter Gray, research professor at Boston College, writes about what he considers to be the problem with education in America, and I think it applies equally to the UK:

> In school, children learn quickly that their own choices of activities and their own judgments of competence don't count; what matters are the teachers' choices and judgments. Teachers are not entirely predictable. You may study hard and still get a poor grade, because you didn't figure out just exactly what the teacher wanted you to study or guess correctly what questions he or she would ask. The goal in class, in the minds of the great majority of students, is not competence but good grades.[10]

By focusing primarily on grades and exam results, there's a danger the student will miss out on the other things education has to offer: a wide knowledge of the subject being studied, intellectual stimulation and the broadening of the mind. Career opportunities and the material things good grades might bring our kids are not the only important things in life.

But don't let me give you the wrong impression. Even in primary school, Dutch children take official tests twice a year. These focus mainly on literacy and arithmetic. They are considered a necessary evil and kept as low-key as possible. The results of these tests are not shown to the children themselves and are not given to the parents in the form of a report. Parents are allowed only a quick glimpse of them twice a year, during parents' evenings. They help to determine which stream of secondary school education the child will enter at the age of eleven or twelve. Nevertheless, there are no total scores. The children's results are never compiled or compared. As I said, it is literally impossible to be top of the class in Holland.

This noncompetitive attitude is apparent in other aspects of school life, too. When my son came home from his first school sports day, I asked him, without thinking, whether he'd won any of his races. He gave me a very confused look. Hadn't they run races, then? Well, yes, they'd done some running, but he'd waited for his friend so they could cross the finish line together holding hands. It was clear that the focus had not been on winning. In fact, there weren't any winners or losers, and there weren't any medals, trophies or teams either. The children went around the sports field in groups, trying out various activities and challenges, and these included inflatable slides, bouncy castles and tenpin bowling, as well as running, jumping and other athletic activities. It didn't sound anything like the sports days of my youth, where I was marked for life when I literally stumbled at the first hurdle. Even my friends had laughed.

In the OECD's *How's Life* survey of 2015, which measured well-being in the various OECD countries, Dutch children were among the least "pressured by schoolwork."[11] Unsurprisingly, children in the English-speaking countries – Ireland, the US, Canada and the UK – were the most pressured. The Dutch scored highly in the numbers of children "liking school." When all the different factors in the survey were combined, the Netherlands was a clear winner in terms of children's happiness at school.

Perhaps because of the inclusion of vocational schools in the Dutch system, the large majority of children remain in school until the age of nineteen: Only a small percentage leave school earlier than this. Interestingly, Dutch children also scored highly on the Programme for International Student Assessment (PISA), a worldwide survey again conducted by the OECD, in reading, math and science, although Spain and Turkey took the lead.[12] The UK and the US came twenty-sixth and thirty-sixth, respectively. The Dutch system proves that academic achievement is possible without pressuring students to overachieve, and without competition.

Another recent OECD report also concluded that the Dutch system places a premium on high standards. According to the report, "the quality of a school's performance, combined with teaching methods that rely on practice and practical engagement with the imagination of children, are behind Dutch educational success."[13] After leaving school, the Dutch maintain a high level of education: According to the PISA statistics for adults aged between sixteen and sixty-five, the mean proficiency in numeracy and literacy scores placed the Netherlands third, after Korea and Finland.

Rina looks back to her schooling in the US

When I first moved to the Netherlands, it wasn't just about relocating to a different country for the sake of love. It was also about learning a different way to live, one that was gentler on the soul. Because, where I come from, life's a whole lot rougher, a bit more fierce and a lot less forgiving of failure and imperfections. When I left, I was walking away from that, too.

The general story goes like this: The child must be an overachiever to get into a prestigious college, graduate from medical or law school, have a fabulous, high-paying career, get married, have two or three kids, drive a fancy car, go on glamorous vacations and live in the right zip code. How much one accomplishes reflects an individual's self-worth as well as how they are viewed by friends, family and within their community.

Though it was heart-wrenching to read the *Atlantic* article "The Silicon Valley Suicides," about the bright kids killing themselves in Palo Alto, I wasn't all that surprised by it. I, too, come from the San Francisco Bay Area, and I can still vividly recall how intense the pressure was when I was in high school, more than a decade ago.[14]

According to the article, the ten-year suicide rate for those particular high schools is between four and five times the national average. They are located only forty-five minutes away from my own former high school. While I am grateful for the world-class education I received, I could have lived without the immense pressure. I didn't appreciate the mean girls and the constant cheating among the students, including those with the best grades. I'll never forget how one particular horrible yet popular girl picked on a meeker girl and made her give up her completed calculus homework to copy. I wish I'd had the self-confidence to tell on the cheats back then, but I stayed quiet, knowing all too well that snitches weren't liked – by either students or teachers.

The message given to kids is loud and clear: Admission to an elite college is necessary to have a successful, happy life, and it doesn't matter how you get there. Madeline Levine, a child psychologist who practices in the Bay Area and who is quoted in the *Atlantic* article, describes meeting adolescents who would "complain bitterly of being too pressured, misunderstood, anxious, angry, sad and empty." It is often said that the way you as a parent talk to your children becomes their inner voice. In many American households, this inner voice is obsessed with success. Somehow, through the constantly repeated message of having to secure perfect grades and perform impressively in extracurricular activities, high school students are expected to be superheroes. I can still recall how, fifteen years ago, my classmates would size each other up, brazenly demanding which schools you had been accepted into and which had rejected you. I was rejected by two universities. I can only guess that I simply didn't make the cut – my straight As were just not good enough. Or maybe there were just too many candidates like me. Even today, it's difficult to write this down: The weight of feeling completely worthless still hangs over me. Despite offers from three other good universities, I felt I'd failed. I locked myself in my room for three days, not wanting to see the look of disappointment on my parents' faces.

There's a reason Amy Chua's 2011 memoir *Battle Hymn of the Tiger Mother* was and continues to be a bestselling parenting book. While she admitted that a lot of it was her attempt at a joke, many others took her book as their new parenting bible. They wanted their kids to be better than the others, because they saw it as a reflection of who they were as parents. Chua's unabashed honesty is what resonates with so many American and, probably, British parents. She's accomplished what many parents aspire to for their children. Not only is she living proof of the American ideal of high academic achievement – she's an Ivy League-educated lawyer and law-school professor – but her two daughters are super talents, too, and well on their way up the meritocratic ladder. In the Netherlands, on the other hand, as long as you get a passing average at a Dutch grammar school, you're basically guaranteed admission to university. It also helps that it doesn't really make any difference which university you attend. It's more of a matter of where you want to go – a fabulous world city like Amsterdam, or a quieter, more rural refuge like Groningen. Here in the Low Countries, you are allowed to be yourself. And Dutch parents have long realized that the emotional well-being of their children is just as important, if not more so, than any external validation of success.

6

On Discipline

In which Michele doesn't have French children

We are in the south of France for half-term, staying not far from where Ina's classmate Elias and his family are vacationing. The great thing about having school-age kids is their making friends with kids whose parents you'd like to hang out with. We drive down to the coast and spend an idyllic afternoon with them on the tiny island called l'Île des Embiez, a short ferry ride from the town of Six-Fours-les-Plages.

While the parents unpack the picnic and lie down on beach towels, the children splash around in the water. Ina, Elias and his younger sister run back and forth, getting sand in the food and talking loudly. Elias' father, Thomas, jokingly complains about Dutch children being noisy and not having any manners. We ban them from coming within three feet of the beach towels and tell them to quiet down. They move along the beach and start poking at a dead jellyfish with sticks. After that they scramble up a rock face and do something out of our sight that is clearly hilarious, judging by their giggles. None of us makes a move to go and check up on them.

A French family is sitting not far away in the small cove. They have two children with them. The adults are resting on deck chairs, the children are sitting on a beach towel about eight or nine feet in front of them. The children don't run, or jump, or shout the entire time we're there. They just sit quietly. While I'm thinking how much more fun our kids are having, Thomas looks over at them and says in his typically dry way, "I wish I had French children." A discussion ensues about how other Europeans envy French parents their perfectly behaved kids. (Obviously, it's one of the key selling points of Pamela Druckerman's *Bringing Up Bébé*.) Dutch children, on the other hand, are notorious abroad for running around restaurants, shouting at the top of their voices and disturbing other diners. Foreigners often find them rude and a bit disrespectful. French parents are more authoritarian and expect children to behave like adults. In the Netherlands, there's a more realistic expectation of what children are capable of and much greater tolerance. Dutch parents tend to be authoritative rather than authoritarian.

I'm pretty sure that one of the things that contributes to the running-around-restaurants-screaming is that Dutch children in the Netherlands are welcome *everywhere*. It's a much more child-friendly, child-centered culture. Cafés and restaurants consciously cater to families. Most of them have play corners with books, puzzles and games. Not that everyone is happy about this. In fact, children running wild in restaurants has even led a pressure group to lobby to introduce child-free restaurants so that diners can eat in peace! A recent article in *Het Parool*, an Amsterdam newspaper, described the issue as "a very Dutch phenomenon: people taking their kids along and leaving them to their own devices."[1]

When, later in the summer, I visit London with Ina, I'm struck by how many places I *can't* take her, especially in terms of bars and restaurants. You can't just pop into the nearest pub. You have to make a concerted effort to find a family-oriented one. Ina's spontaneous bursts of energy as she skips through the crowds on Mare Street in Hackney seem out of place in a country where there's still a lingering sense that children should be seen and not heard. The same is true on vacation in France, where she receives disapproving glances from the saleswoman as she runs around an old-fashioned milliner's shop, exclaiming in wonder at the hats.

In the Netherlands, children are encouraged to act spontaneously. Play is more important than being quietly obedient. The Dutch believe in inspiring children to explore the world around them and to learn from that. Play can be noisy and disruptive to other people, something the French would not tolerate and Brits and Americans might disapprove of. The French children on the beach didn't seem to be playing, so I wondered what were they learning. They weren't investigating the texture of a jellyfish or the slipperiness of loose rocks. They weren't any bother to the adults, but at what cost?

Of course, in the past, parents disciplined their children more – physical discipline was common in Holland until the middle of the twentieth century, as it was in other countries. What to think of the tradition of St. Nicholas' Moorish servant, Black Pete? He was used, up until two generations ago, as a threat for naughty children: He carried a bundle of twigs to flog them with and a burlap sack for taking the "bad" children back to Spain. My mother-in-law, who was as picky an eater as a child as my own daughter, Ina, also comes to mind. According to her elder sister, she got a smacked bottom every single night for not eating her dinner. Did the Dutch use to be disciplinarian, then? What changed?

In 1530, the Dutch philosopher Erasmus wrote a book, *De civilitate morum puerillium libellus*, containing instructions on the education of children. After spending time at a very strict French university with punitive teaching methods, he developed a strong aversion to unforgiving, righteous styles of education. Children's innate, natural aversion to violence and war should be cultivated, he advised, and discipline should be based on encouraging, praising and shaming, rather than flogging. Yet in the past, Dutch schools were strict environments. My own children tell me about an amusing historical form of punishment they learned about, the *pechvogel* – literally, the "unlucky bird" – a stuffed toy bird the teacher would chuck at naughty students. The pupil in question had to return the bird to the teacher, at which point they'd be whacked with a *plak* – a wooden paddle. (Today, the word *pechvogel* is used to describe an unlucky person.) Nevertheless, the Netherlands was one of the first countries to forbid corporal punishment, outlawing it early in 1820.[2]

The American parenting expert Benjamin Spock had great influence on Dutch child-rearing in the postwar period. The Dutch, who had long valued childhood, leapt at his more relaxed approach and his incitements to let children enjoy their innocence and act spontaneously and freely.[3]

When Rina and I talked to historian Els Kloek, she agreed that parents used to be stricter; in the olden days, children had to stand at the table during meals and weren't allowed to speak: "Father's word was law." She said the youth revolution of the 1960s turned everything on its head. Suddenly, it was all about permissiveness and anti-authoritarianism. The Flower Power movement caught on even more in the Netherlands than in Britain, perhaps because there was less of a class system to disassemble. Els was born in the 1950s and says her generation criticized their authoritarian parents and began experimenting by giving great freedom to their children; nothing was forbidden and they had to discover for themselves where the boundaries lay and what was dangerous. This permissiveness probably went too far, she says, citing the absurd case of a couple who took their child, who wouldn't listen to them, to the doctor to have his hearing tested, rather than accepting that their child was simply disobedient.

Today's generation has *reintroduced* rules, boundaries and structure for its children, but within limits. Discipline is not punishment based. For the Dutch, it is about teaching socially appropriate behavior. In a society without a strong social hierarchy, deferring to your elders or betters is a foreign concept, so you don't get the kind of polite deference from children that you might get in France – or in Asia, for that matter. Dutch children are expected to be friendly and helpful toward their elders but not to automatically defer to them. Everyone is on an equal footing. Children are unlikely to be willfully disobedient, but they are more likely to stand up and fight their corner. Learning to put forward a good argument is seen as a useful life skill and so encouraged.

Dutch parenting experts chiefly recommend that adults set a good example so that their child will copy them. Two common expressions translate as "Parenting is practicing what you preach" and "What the old cock crows, the young cock learns." Experts also advise parents not to *ask* a child to do something, but to *tell* them, to say firmly, "I want you to. . . ." The idea is to not give the child a choice of options but to give clear directions. Discipline is not about forcing your child to do things, or getting into power struggles with them, spying on them or checking up on them, threatening them, screaming or shouting. Instead, desirable behavior should be reinforced with praise; unacceptable behavior should be stopped firmly and immediately. Any punishment should be relatable to the particular instance of misbehavior; for example, a child should be asked to repair something they've damaged or tidy up a mess they've made. Other more general recommended punishments are being sent early to bed, or being banned from watching a favorite TV show.

A few weeks after our French holiday, I go round to Thomas and Heleen's house for a chat about discipline. But before we even get

Triple "P" Positive Parenting

The Australian Triple "P" Positive Parenting, an evidence-based parenting program endorsed by the World Health Organization to prevent psychosocial problems in children, is widely promoted by the Dutch government.

Triple "P" has five basic principles:[4]

1. Create a safe and engaging environment.
2. Create a positive learning environment.
3. Use assertive discipline.*
4. Have realistic expectations.
5. Take care of yourself as a parent.

*Here is the description of assertive discipline on its website:

> Contrary to what some people might think, *discipline* is not a bad word. In fact, discipline in a safe, secure, predictable and loving environment can help your child learn to: accept rules, develop self-control, consider others when expressing their feelings, and promote an awareness that their actions have consequences. Assertive discipline means that, as a parent, you:
>
> ◊ Prepare in advance.
> ◊ Set ground rules.
> ◊ Give clear and calm instructions.
> ◊ Praise good behavior.

started, there's a culture clash. They don't seem to understand what I'm asking about; I have to clarify what I even mean by discipline. They don't automatically associate the word with children, even though the

Dutch have the exact same word, pronounced slightly differently. Its definition in the Dutch dictionary is "obedience to regulations and orders," but Heleen's first associations are with self-discipline, in terms of getting her work done, and then sport. The idea of training children to obey orders and punishing them if they transgress is anathema to a Dutch parent. A Dutch parent would usually use the word *opvoeding*, where other British parents might use the word *discipline*. *Opvoeding* means upbringing, raising, rearing, parenting. Implicit in this is teaching a child what's right, through showing not telling, explaining not punishing.

Heleen, who works as a screenwriter, comes across as a confident and competent woman. She tells me that discipline as such isn't high on her parenting agenda; she considers her main task as a parent to be making sure her children are nice people. They should be friendly and responsible above all else, though she does want them to be able to distinguish between right and wrong. Thomas, a cabinet-maker, is usually quicker to let his exasperation show. He jokes about the idea of old-fashioned discipline and meek, obedient children. For him, though, parenting is a journey he takes the children on to show them the great things in life. "It's about giving them opportunities, choices. But, even as an intermediary, I'm often frustrated. They don't always like what I'd like them to like!' Still, he doesn't try to force things on them. What will be will be. Together, Heleen and Thomas look for balance: If their child stays indoors on Friday, they encourage him to play outside on Saturday. They confess that their main struggle is controlling screen time. They have come up with a rule that Elias has to practice his guitar before he's allowed on the computer. Their main form of punishment consists, logically, of removing privileges: screen time for Elias, and bedtime attention for his younger sister, Ruby.

I don't usually think of Dutch people as having particularly good manners. There certainly aren't the formalities that exist in Britain. Yet Heleen brings up the subject of politeness. "Manners are important, but for practical reasons," she says: "to help social interaction. 'Please' and 'thank-you' are essential." Thomas tells me he wants his children to sit up straight at the table and use their knife and fork properly. "Good manners also apply to cycling – it's antisocial to cycle on the pavement."

I ask them to sum up typical Dutch parenting for me.

Heleen says, "It's putting things into perspective. And positive parenting. I don't necessarily agree with it, but there's a great avoidance of the word *no*. Parents will say, 'Would you mind not doing that?' The trend is to appeal to your kids' reason, not to impose things on them."

Thomas adds, "Conflict between parent and child is seen as something to be avoided. It's always softened by consultation, by the parents talking everything through with their kids. . . . But this does mean that, as adults, they have trouble accepting criticism. They can dole it out all right, though. As a child, it doesn't matter what they do; they're always told it's good." Heleen says, "It's typically Dutch to say, 'I've done my best.' Even if you haven't. The Dutch aren't good at self-criticism. Look at our football team!" Thomas adds: "That's why they always lose to the Germans!"

Most Dutch parents agree on basic rules of behavior with their children. The common advice is to have clear rules but to make sure they are in keeping with what the child is capable of. Rules are there to provide structure and boundaries and, if they are broken, there is more likely to be discussion and persuasion than punishment. American parenting expert Elizabeth Hartley-Brewer, in *Positive Parenting* (1991), bemoaned the previous decades of permissive, child-centered parenting. By "[rightly] rejecting strict discipline," she writes, parents also "threw away their authority and responsibility." Like her, the Dutch rediscovered the need for clear rules and boundaries. Now, instead of parents imposing rules on their children, the children are invited to think responsibly about what those rules might be. It's a fine line. For

Dutch parents, responsibility and a good relationship are desirable; authoritarianism is not.

The backlash

In the early summer, a controversial book, *Waarom? Daarom!* (Why? Because I said so!), caused a lively debate in Holland. Its author, Roué Verveer, who was brought up by strict Surinamese parents, takes Dutch parenting to task for not being firm enough. "Stop asking the kids whether they want spinach or broccoli, teach them to eat what they are given!" he writes. His general criticism is that Dutch parents negotiate with their children too much and soften any blow, leaving them unfit for the real world. One reviewer backed Verveer, arguing, "Your child is not your friend." She, too, called for a heavier hand – more old-fashioned discipline, in other words.[5]

But other Dutch parenting experts countered that children learn social and moral behavior by example, not through the threat of being punished. According to research by Leiden University educationalist Rianne Kok, children learn to control their emotions and behavior more effectively through explanation and diversion or distraction than through an authoritarian or punitive style of parenting.[6] Punishment will cause a child to adapt their behavior to avoid the punishment but not to learn what they have done wrong.

Recent research at the Child Study Centre at Manchester University has shown that playing to a young child's strong sense of fairness and justice works better as a behavior strategy than getting angry or punishing them. Erasmus was right all along. And findings indicated that when children witnessed "third-party violations" – offenses against other people – they were more inclined to offer help to the victim than think about punishing the perpetrators.[7] Appealing to a child's natural sense of empathy can be a strong motivational force for good behavior. This is the gentle, understanding approach adopted by Dutch parents.

Rina on the art of reasoning with a toddler

"Julius, it's time for bed," instructs my husband, Bram. "Ten more minutes, Papa. Ten more minutes," responds Julius, looking up from his iPad screen. He's engrossed in *The Monster at the End of this Book*, an interactive read-along book featuring the lovable, furry *Sesame Street* Muppet Grover. The general premise of the book is to do exactly the opposite of what Grover is pleading the reader not to do, which is to turn the page. Julius is obviously having a lot of fun with it. But it's already 6:00 PM and, because of the short winter days, it's completely dark outside. Baby Matteo is getting restless, and we've all had a long, tiring day. "OK, just ten more minutes, Julius. I'm going to time it," says my husband. My husband strategically gives himself a cushion of an hour to get Julius to bed. We clean up the kitchen together, yelling out, "Eight more minutes!" "Five more minutes!" "Three more minutes!" Bram goes to stand in front of Julius, letting him know that it's nearly time. Julius just manages to get to the end of his book in time and looks up, pleased with himself. "All done, Papa! Ready!"

They hold hands as they walk up the stairs. This is only the beginning. The back-and-forth haggling continues: about brushing his teeth, how many books to read, what pajamas to wear, when to turn off the light, and when to finally close his eyes.

This whole negotiation approach can be exhausting; sometimes, it's infuriating. And I admire my husband's patience: His voice remains calm and steady and he stands his ground while our three-year-old attempts to reason his way out of bedtime. It's something I don't find so easy. We are bringing the famed "polder model" into our home (derived from the old way of managing the polders: low-lying land reclaimed from the sea and susceptible to flooding. Because everyone in the community had to pull together to keep the sea out, people found a way of setting aside their differences and coming up with a solution for the greater common good – in other words, decision-making by consensus). Everyone in the family, including the youngest, has a say. Consensus and compromise make for a happy home. And Dutch children will grow into Dutch adults, and in the workplace in the Netherlands anyone and everyone is entitled to their own opinion.

At three years old, Julius has already developed adequate language skills to express what's important to him. Now, it's about teaching him how to formulate his own solutions, but ones that are acceptable to both us and him; it's about learning and practicing how to rationalize. It isn't easy. By allowing our three-year-old child to negotiate, we're teaching him how to set his own boundaries. When Julius questions our authority, he's simply trying to exert ownership of his own life, tell us what he is and isn't comfortable with. It's a skill that will be useful when he's older, whether it's to resist succumbing to peer pressure, to cope when he finds himself in a possibly dangerous situation or asserting himself at work. We do have a common set of rules when it comes to negotiating. As parents, it's important that we explain our position clearly, letting him know, for example, the reason why he has to go to bed early ("So you can get plenty of rest and grow up strong like all the tall Dutch people"). In return, we expect our son to come up with his own arguments. He knows we must all remain respectful – no name-calling, rudeness or interruptions. And, for his part, he can expect us to remain calm, level-headed and patient. Once a compromise has been reached, we move forward and agree to the terms.

Negotiation-based parenting isn't for the faint of heart. It can be exhausting, and your patience will be tested. Although, sometimes, it is maddening to try to have a rational argument with a toddler, we wouldn't have it any other way. It's important to note, however, that in true authoritative parenting style, there are clear, defined boundaries. Within those boundaries, there are lots of freedoms, and things are open to negotiation. For example, Julius' current bedtime is seven o'clock, and he understands this. What he does in between the time he starts getting ready for bed at six till when he falls asleep is where there's flexibility.

Being opinionated and direct is synonymous with being Dutch; it's also why they're one of the happiest groups of people in the world. And they have to start somewhere. It might as well be in the safe, nurturing environment of home.

7

Biking through the Rain

In which Michele lengthens the leash

I'm cycling along the bike path that runs from the park opposite our house to the white monstrosity of the Boven 't Y shopping center. The children's primary school is located right behind it, about a half mile away from our house. I chat to Heleen, while keeping an eye on Ina, who is riding some way ahead of us, next to Heleen's son, Elias. It is busy on the wide bike path on this clear summer morning. Although the opening times of the various schools are staggered so that children from different schools don't all hit the streets at the same time, there are enough children from our school alone using this route to turn it into an obstacle course: There are mothers lane-hogging on massive *bakfietsen* (cargo bikes), four- and five-year-olds pedaling furiously and swerving across the road, and older boys racing along, hands-free. Holland has flat roads with bike paths, no school buses and limited car parking, so the preferred option for getting to school here is by bike, and this embeds the idea of cycling early into the lives of the Dutch as the main way to get around. There are excellent bike paths on the routes to schools, with low-speed zones in their immediate vicinity, and enormous bike sheds once you get there.

Ina, who is eight, has recently asked whether she can cycle to school on her own, as her elder brother, Ben, has been doing for the past two years. Elias, who is in her class, has been cycling to school by himself for the past couple of months. How this plays out in actual fact is that Elias rides ahead of his mother and younger sister and she keeps an eye on him from a distance. He and Ina have arranged to cycle together, which seems like a good plan to me. As they become more confident, we will gradually let them get further ahead of us, slowly lengthening the parental leash, until they are old enough to be allowed to bike to school unsupervised.

Learning to cycle

I remember my son, Ben, aged four, insisting on cycling to school on his first day of primary school. He was wearing a bright red raincoat, carrying a yellow knapsack and riding a bike that still had stabilizers. It wasn't long before those training wheels came off. There's nothing like other children whizzing past unassisted to motivate a child. You often see a parent with one hand on their child's upper back or shoulder, pushing them along and gently guiding them. While cyclists in other countries rarely make physical contact with each other – partly because it's illegal – one of the most romantic things you see the Dutch do (and there aren't many romantic things they do) is to cycle holding hands, or with the woman clasping the man's wrist.

Dutch children seem to spend their entire lives on their bikes. There is a very casual approach to parents cycling with babies, which looks rather like extreme bravery or foolhardiness to outsiders. From a young age, babies are worn in slings as their parents go about their daily business on wheels. It took me a while to get over my nerves and brave a few short trips to nearby baby swimming lessons with my son dangling in front of me, a massive smile on his face and the wind ruffling his hair.

As they get older, children are transported through traffic in a child seat (up front for older babies, on the back for toddlers), or in the royal comfort of a *bakfiets*. We bought a rather pricey two-wheeler *bakfiets* when Ina was a baby and Ben was three, after dithering between a more stable but heavier three-wheeler and the more maneuverable two-wheeler. My husband sometimes has a rather un-Dutch taste for luxury (I blame his foreign genes: He's half Hungarian, a quarter German) and went for a top-of-the-line über-hip sky-blue model.

Our new carrier bike was heavy and wide and took courage to master. But after a couple of weeks I was able to emulate those strapping Dutch mothers and was unfazed by pushing a heavy load of children and a week's grocery shopping. It takes practice and thighs of steel, particularly over the humpbacked bridges, but you get there in the end. While unwieldy in traffic, carrier bikes are extremely practical in places with a good cycle network.

Visitors from abroad often joke about the large collection of bicycles parked behind our front hedge. When my children became too heavy to transport in the *bakfiets* – when I turned, I'd literally tip over to one side and get stuck, not being heavy enough to provide sufficient ballast – I sold it and bought a parent-and-child tandem. While a *bakfiets* is rather broad, tandems are just long. This makes the tandem a much better option for maneuvering among the cars, trams and tourists in the crowded, narrow streets of central Amsterdam.

The Dutch Union of Cyclists promotes cycling "because it makes you happy and improves your health." Cycling must contribute to the fact that, in the Netherlands, there is a lower rate of childhood obesity than in any other First World country. And it's common knowledge that exercise releases endorphins, which make people happy. Researchers at the University of Utrecht have found that cyclists live longer than people who do not use a bike.[1] They say it adds an average of six months to life expectancy. On an average weekday in the Netherlands, 5 million cyclists, young and old, make 14 million trips on their bikes.[2] There are a million more bicycles than there are people. The much-photographed mega bike parks at train stations are truly colossal, and even then it's often hard to find a free spot to put your bike. There are frequent bike traffic jams during rush hour.

Pete Jordan's *In the City of Bikes* is a treasure trove of information on the history of Dutch cycling (it also provides a wonderful social history of Amsterdam). When he first arrived, Pete did the typical foreigner thing of accidentally standing on a bike path and getting run over by a cyclist. He moved to Amsterdam for its bike culture and was fascinated by the variety of cyclists he saw going by on rickety bikes, and started to conduct his own surveys. He soon realized how normal it was for the Dutch to transport all kinds of objects by bicycle: from heavy suitcases, to furniture, to massive houseplants and, surprisingly frequently, ironing boards.

The Dutch have, historically, been so adept at cycling while carrying heavy objects that, in 1917, a Dutch military bicycle "marching" band was set up in which the soldiers played brass instruments as they pedaled. The Dutch army still has a cycle-mounted fanfare band to this day.[3]

Giving someone a lift on the back of your bike, then, is child's play for your average Dutchie. Backies, or "dinking" (balancing a passenger on the back of your bike) are common in the Netherlands, while it is illegal in many other European countries. In the UK, you can take a passenger only on bikes adapted for the purpose – that is, those with a child seat, or a tandem.[4] Backies allow children to build that crucial traffic awareness from an early age. By the time they get their own bikes, children are accustomed to the sensations of balance, speed and traffic around them. As with all things in a Dutch childhood, gradual, regulated exposure seems to be the key to progress. There's less focus on milestones, on children having to be able to do things by a certain age. Instead, parents watch out for indications that a child is ready for a new step and eager to attempt it. It's the same for potty training and swimming as for cycling: The best progress is made when it is child-led, not parent-pushed.

Rina on biking

In the US, biking is seen as something that is mainly for kids and, when adults do ride, it's mainly as a sport or in a minority subculture. To ride a bike is a lifestyle statement. "It just looks so childish," my friend Michelle, a San Francisco native who came to visit us, commented. "Look at that man in his stylish grey suit and polished brown shoes. He looks like a gentleman. But on the bike, he reminds me of a toddler on wheels." In the Low Countries, however, there's nothing alternative about riding a bike – it's how everyone gets around. Because of the flat terrain and the network of bicycle paths, it's the best, most practical and efficient way to travel. As of yet, I still haven't got a Dutch driver's license. Everything is so easily accessible by bike that I've never felt the need to drive. It's also a great way for me to sneak in some exercise. I am definitely a proud *bakfietsmoeder*, the Dutch equivalent of an American mom with a minivan. For my son's first birthday, we went Dutch and gave him a Wishbone bike that starts as a tricycle and then converts into a two-wheeler. For Dutch people, bikes are almost an extension of their bodies. Letting Julius become familiar with a bike when he was barely walking seemed like the natural thing to do. Getting around on his own bike gives him enormous independence and self-confidence.

Michele learns that cycling teaches grit

Even the Dutch call their country "chilly old Frog land." It rains more often than not, with very regular downpours from September to January. February and June are also often wet. Winter temperatures average between thirty-five and forty degrees Fahrenheit, and there are strong winds. Although wind and rain often make conditions uncomfortable for cyclists, the Dutch simply dress themselves and their children in warm clothes, waterproof coats, pants and rain boots and brave the weather all year round. My husband has always insisted we cycle through snow and blizzards. He told me I'd get the hang of it and I did, eventually. You have to allow a certain degree of slip and slide, and use low gears, if you have them, like in mountain biking. That said, most Dutch bikes don't have gears and use the old back-brake system, so they're not really suitable to ride on snow and ice. Cargo bikes do have gears and are better in those sorts of conditions, since their weight means they have more grip on the road surface.

All-weather cycling is a truly character-forming experience. The first few years I lived here, I became so obsessed with cycling against the wind it became a mental as much as a physical battle. Children who learn to cycle in all weather learn *grit*. They learn that life isn't always sunny and full of rainbows. They learn to face the rain. They learn not to give up. I think it's what tiger mother Amy Chua wanted her children to learn when she insisted that they practice their instruments for hours each day. Cycling to school whatever the weather conditions teaches children resilience, and there is a definite link between resilience and happiness. Researchers from the University of Barcelona found that people who are more resilient are also more likely to report high life satisfaction and better control over emotions.[5]

I have shepherded my drenched children into the house for a strip and a warm bath on many an occasion. If there isn't a choice and it's just something you do, they simply get on and do it. One popular

Dutch parenting book I read says that you shouldn't feel sorry for your children when they struggle into school on their own when it's raining and windy and they have a heavy knapsack. Instead, think how responsible and independent it makes them. The same author suggests that if your child forgets their lunch, you shouldn't take it to them. And you should never drive them to school.[6]

Safety concerns

British and American parents tend to drive their primary school–age children to school because they think it's safer than letting them cycle or walk. Viewed from the gung-ho cycling haven of the Netherlands, this seems to be a worrying obsession with safety that limits bike use. My Dutch friend Anne, who moved to London a couple of years ago, shares her experiences:

> My kids have less freedom here than they would in Amsterdam. Cycling on the road by themselves is too dangerous, unfortunately. The danger here isn't the amount of traffic but that the drivers are not used to having cyclists around them, and the lack of cycling lanes. Also, in Holland, almost every driver is also a cyclist and knows how to think like one.
>
> I do cycle with the kids on the road, but it does make me nervous. I make them wear a bike helmet. When they ask why they can ride a bike without one in the Netherlands, I tell them I would be arrested over here by the Mummy Police if they didn't wear one. I don't wear one myself and some people get really cross with me about it.

In Australia and New Zealand, bike helmets are compulsory, as they are in some states of America. In the UK they are recommended and have been adopted by most. So when I first moved to Holland, I brought with me my helmet, my fluorescent yellow cycling jacket, my reflector clips and my pollution mask. I wore them the first few times I cycled but soon became self-conscious. In the safe haven of the bike lanes, I was an object of ridicule. Later, I made my own children wear helmets, but finally relaxed the rule when other Dutch parents persuaded me that children are more careful when they don't feel protected.

One of the reasons helmets are not compulsory in the Netherlands is that cyclists who do not wear them have been found to act more cautiously in traffic. There is also a feeling that the imposition of a helmet law would put people off cycling (as it has done in Denmark).[7] What's more, the Dutch National Cyclists Union claims that research abroad has shown no reduction in head injuries when cyclists wear helmets. Most injuries are caused either by being run over by cars, which causes a different type of injury, or when the cyclist is riding faster than 12 mph (20 kph, the maximum speed at which helmets have some efficacy in protecting cyclists from head injuries).

Statistically, Dutch people are more likely to die of drowning than in a bike accident, which is probably why they are more cautious around water than in traffic. An English expat friend, Imogen, hearing that we were writing this book, immediately asked whether I'd write about how "un-safety conscious" the Dutch are. Unlike in the US and the UK, there is no health-and-safety policing here. That's obvious: Just look at the way people ride their bikes through traffic with all kinds of things balancing on them. Relatively speaking, of course, it is safer to bike in the Netherlands because of the amazing bike-path network. But you do sometimes see parents balancing more than one small child on bikes without child seats – it's like a traveling circus. They are simply more relaxed about the risks. (There are other things that strike you if you come from a more safety-conscious country. The Dutch let off fireworks in the streets on New Year's Eve – something I still find terrifying – giant hogweed grows all over the place, and everyone swims outdoors without worrying about Weil's, the water-borne bacterial disease spread by rats.)

Luckily, according to the body that conducts research into traffic safety, the number of young children killed while cycling is extremely low.[8] Mortality rates have dropped significantly since the 1950s because of the creation of safer cycling lanes and routes. In 1978 Stop de Kindermoord (Stop Child Murder) lobbied for safer cycling conditions for children and organized a demonstration in Amsterdam, with 15,000 cyclists attending. Around the same period, other groups, such as the counterculture Provos and the National Cyclists Union, were also clamoring for better cycling conditions. Separate cycling paths were laid, bike bridges over various canals built and bike racks introduced. The country began to restrict motorized traffic in cities and towns. The infrastructure was so improved by the mid-1990s that there were 29 percent more cyclists in Amsterdam and motorized traffic decreased by 24 percent.[9]

The history of Dutch cycling has had its ups and downs, but cyclists have always won out. Bicycles may have been invented elsewhere – the only part the Dutch invented was the mudguard – but the Dutch have been world leaders in creating a good biking infrastructure. The first bike path was built on the Maliebaan, the largest thruway in Utrecht, as long ago as 1885. Although cycling began as a leisure activity, the depression years of the 1930s saw cheap and practical cycling become the standard mode of transport in the Netherlands.

By contrast, only around 8 percent of the UK population cycles, and only 2 percent of children aged between five and ten, and 3 percent aged between eleven and fifteen cycle to school.[10] Over recent years, London has tried to make itself more appealing to cyclists, and there have been initiatives such as Cycle Superhighways. Some of my old friends have taken up cycling with a passion, and others have been attempting to cycle with their children to school. Yet bike lanes in the UK are often inadequately separated from the traffic, and at various points "run out" into the main traffic lanes, and fatal accidents are still headline news. It is to be hoped that as more and more people get on their bikes, fewer will drive cars, until the cycling movement reaches a critical mass and the streets become safe for bicycling children. But that still seems a long way off; Britain, in this regard, has plenty to learn from the Netherlands.

Toward independence

As we cycle along behind Ina and Elias, Heleen and I compare notes. Heleen tells me that, last week, she let Elias go to the toy shop on his own after school. She felt anxious about it and, after an hour had passed, she decided to go out and look for him. At that precise moment, he arrived home. He'd taken his time, but his first solo trip had turned out fine. Heleen confides in me that she finds the process of letting go somewhat stressful. I agree completely. Yet, teaching our children independence is crucial to enable them to develop into self-sufficient young people. It also lightens the load: If you don't have to ferry your children to and from school and to all of their various clubs and activities, you are less likely to become a time-poor, stressed and overwhelmed parent. You'll be happier, more relaxed and better able to give your child your full attention when they need it.

At this moment, there is nothing we can do to prevent our children from having an accident on their bikes because we are too far behind to intervene. But we are close enough to be on the spot very quickly. This allows the children to develop their own reactions to risk situations and not just blindly follow the adults. Again, this mirrors the advice in Dutch parenting books to learn to let go of your anxieties and allow children to make their own mistakes. If children cannot gain real-life experience, they will never be able to face the difficulties of the traffic on their own. The same can be said about general "street wisdom": Let your children deal with potentially dangerous situations, then they will learn how to assess risks and avoid trouble when they are out and about.

By the time Dutch children go on to secondary school, which is usually much further away from home than their primary school, they are already used to cycling through moderate traffic or on busy bike lanes. Most primary schools run a cycling-proficiency program in the final or penultimate year so that when children start cycling longer distances, they have been trained to deal with the traffic. They will also have taken a theory test and know all the traffic rules and signs. In addition, there are sponsored bike days when all children take their bikes to school and the ANWB (the Dutch traffic association) checks their brakes, lights, reflectors, and so on, and awards certificates. Volunteer parents are brought in to help repair the bikes where necessary.

Cycling even further – secondary schools

A couple of months after my bike ride with Heleen, Ben starts secondary school. He has gotten into his first-choice school – a modern *gymnasium* with a focus on film and drama studies. It's about a half-hour cycle from our house and he'll have to take the ferry over the IJ river. Funnily enough, his big day starting at his new school coincides with that of King Willem Alexander's eldest daughter, Princess Amalia. As Ben sets off on his Batavus bike, wearing jeans and a hoodie and carrying a heavy knapsack of books, the news features a short clip of Amalia, also setting off unaccompanied on her Batavus, also wearing jeans and a hoodie. She looks like every other Dutch child going up to big school. I'm worried about Ben, but surely no more worried than the king and queen are about their eldest child.[11]

Cycling royals are a regular sight. Queen Wilhelmina used to cycle around The Hague in the 1930s, and around London, when the Oranjes (the royal family) lived there in exile during the Second World War. When she returned to the Netherlands after the war, she toured the country on her bicycle, assessing the needs of the people during the postwar reconstruction period. Her daughter Juliana followed suit, and if you google Willem Alexander (the current king) + bike, there are numerous publicity shots of him and his wife and children cycling. Some shots feature a carrier bike filled with their blond, smiling children. It's clear that, for the Dutch, a bike is not a poor man's car, but the best mode of transport for all.

A mysterious lesson called ACT appears on Ben's online schedule for his second week of school. To my pleasant surprise, it's the first of a couple of special lessons on road safety around the school. The children are divided into groups, according to which direction they cycle in from. Then they mark out on a map any dangerous intersections or obstacles on their route to school, photograph them and discuss how they could be made safer. Their suggestions are compiled and sent to the local council. It's fantastic: They have been made more aware of the dangerous points in their journey and learned to be proactive in dealing with them.

Of course, now that Ben is setting off on his own every day in the opposite direction, Ina is starting to clamor for cycling independence of her own. I suggest that she cycle with Elias more often, or with other classmates who ride the same route. On the weekend, she wants to cycle to a friend's house, but she isn't a hundred percent sure of the way. "Why don't you let me cycle ahead, Mummy?" she suggests, "and then you can tell me if I go wrong." I cycle along behind her, reminding her halfway there of "the lifesaver," that final check over your shoulder as you turn left. When we get to the estate where her friend lives, the main street is barricaded off for construction works. She instinctively makes her way around it, taking an additional left and a right and coming at his street from the opposite end. At her age, I would have been a lot more flustered to have had to work out an alternative route, but she handles it all beautifully.

How to cycle while carrying an umbrella

1. Practice cycling one-handed, and particularly negotiating bends, junctions and humpbacked bridges.
2. Buy a very strong, windproof umbrella.
3. Walk around with your umbrella in strong winds. Move your wrist in a snake-like fashion to ensure the umbrella never catches the wind like a sail.
4. Repeat the above, but on your bike.
5. Repeat the above, but on your bike during a storm.
6. Repeat the above, but while also transporting an infant, an ironing board and a houseplant.

8

A Childhood of Freedom

*In which Michele doesn't get arrested for
letting her children play outside*

Working Mom Arrested for Letting Her 9-Year-Old Play Alone at Park – A South Carolina woman thought it was better than forcing her kid to sit at McDonald's all day. Now the state has taken custody.

—*Atlantic*, July 15, 2014

NORTH TRURO – Two Niagara Falls, New York, residents will be arraigned in November on charges that they left two children, ages 7 and 9, alone for an hour in August on a public beach, according to Orleans District Court records.

—*Cape Cod Times*, October 29, 2015

Perhaps you are familiar with the painting *Children's Games* by Pieter Brueghel the Elder (1560). It depicts a street corner dotted with dozens of children at play, more than two hundred in all. The houses look solid but the street is compacted mud; there are no cobblestones. You see the children's toys – stilts, a hobby horse, a doll, jacks, and a hoop and stick – and the games they play: leapfrog, blind man's bluff, hide and seek. Children climb trees and do handstands, clambering on a pile of sand behind the houses; little girls twirl round in circles, making their skirts fly out. More than eighty different games have been identified. But I can't see any parents in the painting. Are those teenagers or adults riding a barrel in the foreground? Are there any adults at all watching over these free-spirited children? It doesn't seem so. There is just one woman, throwing a blue cloak over some children who are huddled together – but it looks like she's joining in the fun.

Brueghel showed that, for children, play is just as important and absorbing as work is to adults. In the sixteenth century the debate about the importance of play was just heating up. The humanists, led by Erasmus, actively encouraged outdoor play all year round – unsupervised play. There were a few restrictions – children weren't allowed to play in churches or graveyards, or make a racket out in the street – but otherwise, in their free time they had free rein.

Foreigners visiting the Low Countries in the seventeenth and eighteenth centuries were surprised by how much consideration was shown to children and how much they were valued by their parents. The Swiss naturalist and physiologist Albrecht von Haller, visiting Leiden in 1723, wrote *"Die Jugend ist ungeschliffen"* (The youth is spoiled).[1] He thought the children were rude and ill-bred; they had too much freedom and were cheeky to their elders. Visitors to the Netherlands are rather likely to say the same things today. A typical park or playground scene still resonates with the chaos that can be seen in Brueghel's painting.

Where I live, in front of our row of semidetached and terraced houses is a broad pavement covered in makeshift garden furniture, sandboxes, wading pools and parked bikes. It's an obstacle course. Since the majority of the houses are inhabited by young families, it's almost impossible to walk along our pavement: In the summer, our neighbors are likely to move their entire sitting rooms out onto the street. They don't think twice about carrying out their sofas, dining tables and armchairs, making the most of the infrequent sunshine. I've even seen coffee tables hosting televisions cabled out through the window. The youngest children play here with a whole array of toys: chalk, water toys, tricycles, dolls and cars. Their mothers may sit outside chatting away, drinking coffee, or breastfeeding; or they are invisible inside, getting on with whatever they have to get on with.

Our street runs alongside a large, landscaped park. The Noorderpark forms a long vertical strip through the neighborhood, embracing the west and east banks of a shipping canal. Our row of houses is built on the bank of a dike. From the street, it looks like they are two-story houses but, once you're inside, you discover stairs leading down to a basement, which opens onto the back garden. This is typically Dutch – modest-looking on the outside, but the houses suddenly open up, Tardis-like, when you're inside. The back gardens are tiny due to the shortage of land. Some families use them mainly for storage; others as a place where the parents can go for a bit of peace and quiet. I can't help thinking it's their size that might have led to the creation of communal recreation areas at the front of houses and the building of playgrounds in the cities.

There are small playgrounds on almost every street corner in Amsterdam. The city has around 1,300 in total, the first being built in 1880. After the Second World War, many more were added; later, the increase in the number of cars on the streets left children with nowhere safe to play outside. Architect Aldo van Eyck designed 860 of them, inspired by urban modernism. Standard attributes were a metal domed climbing frame, parallel bars, a slide and a spring rider. There is one of these around the corner from us. These days, the trend is to build more natural adventure playgrounds, with tree trunks, wooden climbing areas, sand and water. The idea is that children should be allowed to get mucky. Our park has a perfect example, complete with mud; it often becomes an aqua playground, since it floods frequently and the entire construction can be knee-deep in water.

So, back to my street. While the babies crawl along the pavement and toddlers mess around in front of the houses, older children, from the age of four or five, start crossing the road to play in the park opposite. There they climb a crooked tree, which my son has fallen out of several times. He can't be the only one; it's been a firm favorite of all the neighborhood children for years. No one would think of fencing it off or putting down a protective rubber surface underneath. There is also a wading pool (with a supervisor), a big grassy field and a sandbox. One rarely sees a parent in the park but, in general, there are a lot of kids. How does this work?

Outdoor play is still a very normal part of Dutch childhood, just as it was in Brueghel's day. It's a part of the Dutch character to go outside in all weather. Children will happily play outside in the rain. Sporting activities are rarely canceled due to bad weather. The only time Ina's twice-weekly football training doesn't go ahead is if there's a risk of lightning hitting the field. If it's wet, the Dutch wear anoraks. If they're wearing nice clothes they learn to cycle carrying an umbrella in one hand. "There's no such thing as bad weather, only bad clothing," Dutch parents say, unflappable, hardy and prepared for anything. Children are expected to be the same. Given an equal role in the family, children are taught to be self-sufficient and accept responsibility at an early age. Playing outside unsupervised is a rite of passage that teaches them independence and toughens them up.

Dutch culture is suffused with the idealized image of a child who is rosy-cheeked from outdoor fun, their blond hair mussed up.

Independent outdoor play is seen as the antidote to breeding passive, media-addicted couch potatoes. The Dutch believe that children need to be let out to run each day, like dogs. Though some of our neighbors' kids started younger, my two have been playing independently in the park since the age of six. When I started investigating the advice Dutch parents were given in books, one, whose title translates to "And if we just started parenting normally again," came up repeatedly. It outlines a moderate parenting approach with some structure and discipline, but room for unsupervised play:

> As soon as a child approaches four years old, he reaches the age of being able to play "outside." And "outside" means no longer just in the garden but also out on the square, in the sandbox next to the climbing frame, in the alleyways between the houses, on the pavement and so on . . . entirely alone and out of sight of his mother.[2]

The authors, Feddema and Wagenaar, go on to argue that horsing around with other children without parental supervision is good for a child's social development. They will learn to argue and to solve problems by themselves. Parental anxiety, or parents hovering or constantly checking up on them, can negatively affect children, making them nervous and wary. It is better to simply give them clear rules before they go out and insist on good timekeeping, the authors advise. Unwittingly, I'd done this myself, by giving mine the kitchen timer, set to forty-five minutes, when they ventured into the park alone, because I didn't feel they could be relied on to check their watches. The standard advice is for parents to initially keep a discreet eye on the children, but without interfering. I would watch mine through our bay windows.

Research has shown the social benefits of letting children play outside together. Lia Karsten, an urban geographer at Amsterdam University, has found that, in cities, "strict parental accompaniment from A to B by car or by bike leads to 'social impoverishment,' because, unlike in the past, it means that children won't mix with children from other social classes on the street. In villages, this is still possible: The farm laborer's kids will play with the doctor's kids on the village square."[3] It is true that most liberal-minded Dutch parents I know believe in letting their children mix with others from different social and ethnic backgrounds.

Dutch parents believe in giving their kids the freedom to roam, even if it means that they may fall down and hurt themselves. This is what Professor Ruut Veenhoven called "independence training" when he was explaining to Rina and me what he thought made Dutch kids happy. He told us it was wrong to try to curtail or protect kids too much: They must learn to fall down and pick themselves up again. "If they never fall, they never learn to avoid it," he added. Allowing them to be bored is also important; how else can a child learn to play on their own? A parent's job is not to entertain them constantly; the kids need to find ways to occupy themselves and invent their own amusements – that will stimulate their creativity and ingenuity. If they don't learn this, they'll turn out like that friend of Selma's son in London: bored after half an hour in a house filled with toys and young friends.

Rina's take on free-range parenting

The day we moved into our cottage last summer was the day we welcomed a more free-range parenting approach. The wrap-around garden is encircled by a fence and has a trampoline, a sandbox, trees and bushes to play hide-and-seek in, and plenty of grass to roll around on. We didn't need to worry about keeping Julius entertained. He was transfixed by all the children passing by our home, some as young as five years old, biking and playing out on the streets without adult supervision. After checking to make sure he would be safe and secure, we left Julius alone in the gated garden to help the removal company to unpack and get our house set up. Bram and I would take turns checking up on him every ten minutes or so. Julius would also go in and out of the house, completely beside himself with his newfound freedom. In the US or the UK, chances are we could have gotten in serious trouble with the law if one of our neighbors had decided to report us. These days, Julius spends a lot of time playing in the garden unsupervised.

Ironically, many of today's American parents enjoyed a very different childhood themselves, with unlimited freedom to ride their bikes and play in the parks, streets and woods without a parent hovering by. In 2015, President Obama signed off on a federal law that states that children should be allowed to travel to and from school on foot, by bus or by bike alone when their parents have given permission, and that parents should not be exposed to civil or criminal charges for allowing their child to responsibly and safely travel to and from school by a means the parents believe is age-appropriate.[4] However, nothing in this law can preempt state or local laws, so each of the individual fifty states is still able to criminalize parents for such behavior. This means that if your nosy neighbor feels your child is too young to be walking to and from school unsupervised, there's still the chance that they will call the police and Child Protective Services, leading to the possibility of your child being taken away from you, and criminal proceedings being instituted against you, which may lead to your arrest. This would never happen in the Netherlands.

Michele compares notes on play in the UK

During the summer holidays, I take Ina to London and we spend a day hanging out with an old university friend of mine, Vicky, and her two kids. Her son Riley and Ina hit it off instantly. As we sit watching them kick a ball around the play area on Hampstead Heath, we discuss the differences between Britain and the Netherlands. Here, I notice, many of the parents in the playground are hovering over their children or actively playing with them. (I see the same scene later in the week when I visit Victoria Park with my friend Paul and his little daughter, and Paul comments, "You can't let them out of your sight.") Like me, Vicky feels there is too little freedom for kids in the UK. "Riley desperately *wants* to be independent," she says. "He has real issues about it. He's a very articulate seven-year-old and he feels cramped. 'Why can't I go out on my own?' he asks. 'You know where I am, I know where you are . . .' But I can't let him, it's just not done here, even though I would trust him."

She also tells me she was out in the car recently and had to stop for the restroom. "I locked the kids in the car and asked a man standing there to keep an eye on them, yet I felt like what I was doing was probably illegal."

Dutch friends who have moved to London tell me that allowing their children the freedom to learn to behave responsibly doesn't go down too well with the locals. "When our eight-year-old walks home alone she is often stopped on the street. 'Where are your parents? Has anything happened?' What kind of signal is that sending to a child?" a journalist father of three tells me. His wife, my friend Anne, is also unhappy with the situation.

"We have let our eleven-year-old walk to school and back by herself for over a year," she says. "And although friends congratulate us on our independent daughter, you can see the look of horror in their faces. Some say they can understand why we allow her to walk by herself, because she is 'so sensible.' But of course we can allow her to be independent, because we have given her space to try it out: When she first went on little walks by herself, she wasn't scared of being alone, but of grown-ups interfering and asking her why she was by herself. There is a lot more fear of 'bad people' – stranger danger here."

Unbordered freedoms
When I get back home, I happen to see a television interview with Damiaan Denys, a Belgian philosopher and psychiatrist who works

in Amsterdam. He talks about what first attracted him to the Netherlands: "I was impressed by all the unbordered expanses of water, by the total freedom . . . Dutch people teach their children to swim, instead of fencing off the danger." It's a great metaphor. Despite the boundless freedom, he warns that society in general is getting ever more protective: "We now expect rules and regulations to banish all risk. We can no longer deal with our fears."[5]

Parents' pervasive anxiety about their children is something that comes up again when I meet up with my friend and former colleague Madea for a coffee. She and her partner moved to a new housing development in North Amsterdam when their twins were small. They worried about all the things that could happen to the kids: There were deep, open ditches between the houses and a building site behind them. "It was actually quite a suffocating idea that I would have to keep an eye on them all the time," says Madea. "I'm rather a controling mother and I didn't find it easy even to leave them in the crèche one day a week, for example. But we made a conscious decision to let the children play outside without being observed, after we had warned them of the dangers. I think it's really good for kids to be able to do things without their parents always knowing everything."

I asked Paulien, my friend Arwen's mother, what things were like when she was a child in the 1950s. "There was a lot of freedom in my childhood. I grew up in south Amsterdam, near the Amstel River," she tells me. "On Sundays I was free to roam with a bunch of kids."

I asked whether her parents always knew where she was.

"No. We could be in a different part of the city, or swimming in the Amstel, or out on boats. We could come and go as we pleased."

"At what age?" I asked.

"From about four. I walked to school with my elder sister. It was about a fifteen-minute walk. We started cycling to school when we started secondary school. Our bikes were kept in the basement. We couldn't manage to get them out by ourselves before that."

Arwen then started relating her own experiences. As a child, she had to tell Paulien where she was, and with whom. But her parents were fairly relaxed: That was *all* they needed to know. She would go out to play on the village square and in the playground. It was a quiet village. The kids would all hang out in the woods. There was a busy road and they had to be careful crossing it. Paulien chips in, "I taught them to cross the road. I waited until I had seen them doing it properly before I allowed them to do it on their own."

The question of pedophilia comes up, and Paulien says, "It's actually very easy for a person to snatch a child. We always warned them to be wary of strangers. But what are the chances? It's extremely unlikely. We warned them not to take sweets from strangers, and that people sometimes tell lies: Never go off with strangers."

Now living in Amsterdam, Arwen is bringing up her two sons in an urban area that is busier than her quiet, childhood village. She was worried about the danger from cars when the boys were younger and would regularly check where they were when they played outside. But now she says, "I feel it's important that they have the freedom we had as children. Playing out of sight of your parents is important." At eight, her eldest son, Lasse, started cycling to tennis and hockey on his own. He had an old mobile phone so he could call his mother when he left to go home. Now, at ten, he sometimes comes home from school alone and waits for his parents to get back. Grandmother Paulien adds, "You need to give them that sense of responsibility. Otherwise, they'll be so helpless later."

Thinking about this, I realize it's a practical necessity for Dutch children to be independent and self-sufficient by the time they get to secondary school. There are no after-school clubs for that age group, and they are expected to get themselves to and from school and to stay at home alone until their parents get back from work. Arwen's sons have been left home alone for an hour or so during the day since the eldest was nine and the youngest was six. She hasn't yet left them alone in the evening but is planning to next year. She says, "But of course I'd feel terribly guilty if anything ever did go wrong."

In the UK, although there isn't a prescribed legal age under which children must not be left on their own, parents can be and sometimes are prosecuted for leaving their children home alone if it is considered to place them at risk. What constitutes risk is a moot point. A British friend of mine with young kids told me recently that his neighbor had threatened to alert the authorities if he let his six-year-old play on the front porch unattended again. This situation would be considered absurd in Holland.

Paulien tells me that she told her daughters how to get out of the house in case of a fire. Since their bedrooms were in the attic, there was a rope ladder to hang out of the window in an emergency. One time, when the girls were teenagers, she and her husband had gone away to the Ardennes for a weekend, leaving them behind, and the teenage Arwen fell ill. There were no cell phones back then, so the parents weren't easily reachable. But Arwen's sister had the initiative to call the doctor, and they managed to deal with the situation by themselves. Paulien had clearly done a good job teaching them to be sensible and self-sufficient.

Perceived risks

It's true that, these days, in busy city centers in the Netherlands, fewer kids are being allowed to cycle alone and there is a general move toward protecting children a little more. But it's nothing like the over-protective anxiety you find in the US or the UK. Dutch kids' parents played outside unsupervised when they were young, and now they consciously try to allow their children to do the same. So, while the Dutch parents I spoke to do worry about their children playing next to water or in the woods, or cycling on busy bike paths, they try to put their own fears into perspective and not allow them to curtail or restrict their children unreasonably. What might look, from the outside, like easygoing, relaxed parenting is often quite challenging for the parents involved. They have to make a conscious decision to let go of their own fears in the interest of their child. It is not, as I have found, that Dutch parents aren't aware of the risks. They are just as aware as British and American parents, they simply approach risk in a saner fashion.

At my weekly yoga class, the subject of "letting go" comes up. Today the class consists of just three mothers, each with a child about to face a new challenge: an experienced mom whose eighteen-year-old son has just gone off traveling, a young mom whose son is starting primary school, and me with my son about to start secondary school. We compare notes on the forthcoming changes. "Every step they take, we have to learn to let go," the eldest mom says, and she's right.

Equipping children for freedom

Just as all children learn to cycle at an early age and take cycling proficiency tests, in this water-soaked country, more than a quarter of which lies below sea level, there is a strong push for children to learn to swim: There are canals and drainage ditches full of water everywhere. School swimming lessons for every child were introduced after the war. It is normal for all children to take the "A diploma" test by the age of seven or eight. This includes not just being able to swim several lengths of the pool, but also some basic lifesaving techniques, such as swimming with clothes on and diving through a hole in a plastic sheet underwater. It seems a sensible way to equip children for playing safely around water.

I wondered whether many serious accidents resulted from children having the freedom to play outside, so I got in contact with a neurologist, Dr. Janneke Horn, at the Academic Medical Center (AMC) hospital in Amsterdam, who treats head injuries. She tells me most accidents happen in the home. "More people fall down the stairs than anything else. A lot of accidents happen in silly ways." I tell her Ben managed to break his fingers a couple of years ago by falling off the sofa. "Yes, that's quite typical. You know, it's more useful, in terms of accident prevention, to teach your kids to hold on to the bannisters when they're coming down the stairs than to stop them from playing outdoors or cycling."

Germs are, of course, something that today's parents frequently worry about. The Dutch seem much less preoccupied with protecting their children from germs than people in other Western countries today. The first time I saw a Dutch mother picking up a dropped candy from the street and handing it back to her toddler, I was reminded of my own grandmother's insistence that dirt was good for you. Meanwhile, I noticed that German and American expat friends of mine with young children seemed to be obsessed with hygiene. These friends were constantly disinfecting bottles and pacifiers and anything else their kids came into contact with. The Dutch generally believe that if a child picks up some morsel of food or a sweet they've dropped within five seconds, they can put it into their mouth and be all right. Encountering germs is healthy, because children need to build up their immune systems. Not surprisingly, Dutch doctors prescribe antibiotics much less frequently than other countries in Europe and in the US.

But what about actual safety? How safe *is* it out there? On my street, we all know our neighbors will keep an eye on the kids if we don't. At school, the children have information sessions about pedophiles and bullying. They are routinely taught to say, "Stop! *Hou op!*" (Stop it!), and hold up a hand to anyone bullying them. And, significantly, there is no scare-mongering in the media here, while in the US and the UK the tabloids act as paranoid social watchdogs, barking in alarm at anything that might be a matter of public safety, particularly concerning child abuse, abduction and murder.

No wonder people worry about their children. It's a jungle out there, the public are told in the US and the UK. And the government is doing nothing about it. In her excellent historical survey, *Dream Babies:*

Childcare Advice from John Locke to Gina Ford, Christina Hardyment comments on the pervasive alarmism in present-day Britain. Children become not just victims but also predators. There is footage on TV shows of kids from hell, accompanied by tough-love advice. The government cuts spending and blames juvenile delinquency on single moms. And, more than anything, parents are made to feel it's dangerous outside the home:

> We are so bombarded with horror stories, backed up by far from conclusive research, pessimistically presented statistics and hearsay, that it would be easy to believe that we are bringing up our children in the most dangerous, degenerate, and perverted world since time began, rather than the healthiest quarter century in history.[6]

Benjamin Spock is considered the father of the "free-range" parenting movement, which aims to teach children to function independently in an age-appropriate manner. Yet, the revised 1992 edition of his famous childcare manual, *Dr. Spock's Baby and Child Care*, included many new pieces of advice on health and safety issues, reflecting the cultural pressures of the time. Parents were advised to have their tap water tested for bacteria and nitrates; crib slats should be no more than 2⅜ inches apart. As Christina Hardyment reflects, "The safer our world, the more we worry." She also points out that the primary cause of death in babies and infants is car accidents.[7] So why did British parents start ferrying their children to school in the car rather than letting them walk or cycle?

This hyper-safety-consciousness chimes with my stepsister's experience back home. A recent Facebook update from her reads:

> My daughter came home from school today to say they're not allowed to do cartwheels or handstands in the playground

any more. So this adds to the list of things . . . no skipping ropes, no elastic, no bouncy balls, or balls of any description. Obviously, for health-and-safety reasons.

Our generation of Brits grew up playing outside unsupervised, with balls and skipping ropes, stilts and pogo sticks. What went wrong? When I ask her what has caused the paranoia at her school, she surprises me, saying she thinks the school is afraid of being sued. My stepsister receives lots of cold calls from companies offering to assist her in damages claims against third parties, something I believed was common only in the US. Has commercialized litigation become so common in the UK, too, and has it caused this increased caution? Comparing the situation of my stepsister with that in Holland, I remember reading recently that the Dutch are the most insured nation on the planet, after the Swiss. Everyone has personal liability insurance in case they accidentally fall through a painting or knock over a vase. But then again, the Dutch have always had to live crowded together in a small country, hence the polder model of collaboration and consultation. Suing each other would make things very difficult. Is that the reason why the Dutch don't let health and safety concerns prevent their children from having fun?

Pressure to learn

In contrast to the free time Dutch children have, many overscheduled American and British kids don't have much time to play; they may have piano lessons, team practice, homework, drama, ballet, or chess club and after-school tutoring to fit in. Who has time for playdates when all the kids around you are busy building up their résumés to improve their chances of getting into the right school and the right university? Aspirational parents get in the way of a child's happiness, it seems.

The Dutch believe that by cutting out outdoor play you hamper your child's development. Free-range parenting might look like neglect to overanxious, protective parents, but it could be in your child's best interest. According to research stemming from the 1960s, the happiest, most successful children are the ones whose parents let them play where they want to and respect their autonomy, but all the while stay responsive and involved when required.[8]

My children's primary school places emphasis on allowing the kids to play outdoors as much as possible. During the exam week in May, children spend even more time outside. It falls in the same week as the

Ben and Ina's favorite outdoor games

Speklapje is a type of Dutch bacon, but it's also Ina's favorite playground game.

How to play *speklapje*: Begin by choosing some children to be zombies. The other children (the strips of bacon) run away as fast as they can. The zombies try to catch them. When tagged, they become zombies, too. The game ends when there are no "strips of bacon" left.

Ben's favorite playground game is *Ontmoeten of afwijken*, which translates as "Meet or Dodge." Ben explains: "Each child silently chooses another child in the game to focus on, and then decides if they will move toward or away from that child. If you have succeeded in the first round, by catching or dodging your secret opponent, you can go to the next level and choose someone else, again, just in your head. You lose if someone you are trying to dodge catches you, or if you are trying to catch someone and they dodge you and someone else catches you. The two left at the end win."

This game obviously requires a degree of honesty, but Ben assures me that no one cheats.

annual *Avond4daagse*, a nationwide children's walking event in which most primary schools take part. Every evening for four consecutive days, children as young as four gather together to walk five kilometers (about three miles), with the older children doing ten (just over six miles). When I first heard about this, I didn't let my children participate, because it was exam week and I thought they'd be too tired and over-excited to sleep afterward. In subsequent years, I did an about-face. It proved a wonderful distraction for them from exam stress. Ina ran rather than walked her five kilometers with her friends, getting up to all kinds of mischief along the way. It meant the children were calm the next day for their exams, having worked off any excess energy.

From the age of six, my children have gone on overnight school trips. My daughter's most recent one was a resounding success. They had two nights away from home, in a house in the woods, with a visit to a museum, lots of outdoor play, bonfires and the traditional *bonte avond* (cabaret night), at which children are encouraged to perform a turn: sing, dance, tell jokes or do a magic trick. On the last night, there was a disco until midnight at which all the teachers and the headmistress danced along with the children to the latest irritating kid's hit, "Gummy Bear." Ina came home raving about it.

This week, the first week of the school summer holidays, both my children are at Camp Agnes, a traditional weeklong day camp run by volunteers. Any child living in Amsterdam can attend for just thirty-eight euros per week (the equivalent of forty dollars), for any or all of the six weeks of the school summer holiday. It's hard to believe that any kind of childcare can be made available for this price; it's so affordable because it's heavily subsidized by the local authorities, as are many sporting activities.

The Netherlands has a tradition of these holiday day camps for *bleekneusjes* (pale faces) from the city, and children from all backgrounds go to them. They were first established in the 1940s. Run by volunteers, Camp Agnes takes place in the countryside and a base camp is set up next to some woods where the children can play freely. There are no restrictions on climbing trees in this country! Various organized activities are offered, and there is a tent full of games such as shuffleboard, chess and table tennis, as well as playing fields for football and volleyball. Buses drive around the city picking up children from a large number of collection points and bringing them back home again at the end of the day. This solves the problem of summer holidays for working parents in one fell swoop.

The latest research from Cambridge University highlights the risks of *not* allowing children to play freely. "Play is curtailed by perceptions of risk to do with traffic, crime, abduction and germs, and by the emphasis on 'earlier is better' in academic learning and competitive testing in schools," writes Dr. David Whitebread of the Faculty of Education. He continues, "Yet those of us who are involved in early childhood education know that children learn best through play and that this has long-lasting consequences for achievement and well-being."[9]

9

The Simple Life

In which Rina goes camping

"Camping on the farm!" exclaims Julius, over and over again. We're heading toward a campground on an organic goat farm in the country. Our family's been invited to try out de Groene Hoeve (Green Farm) in exchange for a review on my blog. It's only forty-five minutes north of the capital, Amsterdam, but the bucolic surroundings transport us to another time and space.

When my husband first heard about me accepting the offer, he had a good, hearty laugh at my expense. "You? Camping? On a farm? You do understand that means public shower rooms? No room service, or fresh daily bed linen and towels?" But I wasn't going to give up the opportunity of a free weekend getaway.

For the Dutch, going on vacation is an integral part of life. Three times a year is the norm for an average middle-class Dutch family, often for three or four weeks at a time – something that's inconceivable in the UK and even more so for working parents in the US. Everyone is, after all, acquainted with the platitude "Americans live to work and Europeans work to live." And in between these holidays, the Dutch like to get away for long weekends, too.

Having grown up in the (sub)urban jungles of the San Francisco Bay Area, I have very little experience of camping. The idea of it is just something that my conservative, immigrant parents couldn't fathom. Why would you willingly give up the creature comforts of a modern home? For them, vacations were associated with luxury, not with camp fires and sleeping rough.

The first and only time I had been camping was a five-day school retreat at Caritas Creek near Occidental, California, a rite of passage for all eighth graders at my school. While the beauty of nature did leave an impression on me, I did not relish the discomfort of the rustic cabins and the inconvenience of the public shower halls. This time, however, I was more drawn to the idea. I wasn't enthusiastic about the idea of encountering owls and other creatures that go bump in the night. But when I discovered there was a private bathroom for each tent, I was sold. Camping is a Dutch national institution and I worried we were missing out. I wanted Julius to experience what Dutch people consider to be an essential component of childhood.

Once the school holidays start, Dutch people hit the freeways in hordes. The Netherlands Board of Tourism estimates that 850,000 Dutch people set up their tents inside the country and another 1.9 million go camping abroad, the trunks of their cars stuffed full of supplies of Heineken beer, Old Amsterdam cheese, bread, chocolate sprinkles, potatoes, sausages and peanut butter. It's good to have a few creature comforts, and it saves money, too. For good measure, they even bring along their favorite brand of toilet paper. The concept of camping was imported here from the UK, but it took the Netherlands by storm. The first Dutch campsite opened in Vierhouten in Gelderland in 1925. The Dutch caravan manufacturer Kip was established in 1947 and continues to do good business to this day.[1]

During one of our relaxed dinners with two of our dearest Dutch friends, Ewoud and Jop, the topic of camping comes up. I'm constantly asking them to explain the Netherlands; they both have master's degrees in history, so they are well able to tell me all the ins and outs. Fortunately, they're always happy to indulge me in informal "integration" lectures.

"What is it about camping that the Dutch love so much?" I ask, nursing a beer.

"Camping is an economical way to vacation," explains Ewoud, taking another helping of the seafood paella.

"It's because we Dutch people are frugal. Camping is a way to have fun with the family while staying true to the Dutch national pastime of *bezuinigen* – thriftiness," adds Jop.

Thriftiness is a concept that permeates every aspect of Dutch culture and social policy. *Bezuinigen* could almost be counted a spectator sport – it is accepted that one has the right to brag about how much one saves and that others will listen. The Dutch are also cautious when it comes to spending money on gifts and in giving children pocket money. The National Institute for Family Finance even publishes guidelines online, suggesting how much pocket money is appropriate at each age.[2] At first, I thought this Dutch habit of thrift suggested that they were miserly and cheap. It took me more than seven years to grasp that the Dutch are concerned with getting value for money: Camping just happens to be an ingenious way to vacation economically (assuming, that is, that all the gear will be used for several years). I also discovered that the Dutch donate more to charity than any other country in the world and that almost a third of the population does some voluntary work.

But camping isn't solely about saving money: It's also a way of enjoying a change of routine and of living more closely to nature, together as a family. Though recent trends show a slight decrease in camping

– thanks to the availability of cheaper holidays in sunnier climes – camping continues to be popular, as does boating. For the first ten years of Bram's life, his parents would pack him and his three siblings into the family boat and head off on the waterways that crisscross the country. The family boat is an alternative to the family caravan – affordable lodgings for the whole family to enjoy and use year after year. It's all about living the simple life – something the Dutch do often, and well.

A crash course in Dutch parenting

The moment we arrive on the premises, Niki, the farm owner, appears as if from nowhere. She's a middle-aged woman with kind eyes, and long blond hair messily tied in a fashionable bun. She looks like a poster child for the Berkeley organic movement – a natural beauty in touch with Mother Earth.

"It's going to be a bit of a walk," says Niki, as she offers to help carry our many belongings. I'm overequipped, as usual. Because the camp is located on a working farm, it's like a cross between Disney's Animal Kingdom and *Little House on the Prairie*. Grazing just outside our tent are goats and horses, separated from us only by a wooden fence. The tent itself, with a wood-fired stove in the middle and a Dutch cupboard bed, is *gezellig* – cozy and inviting. Julius is ecstatic. Former trips to Paris, Sardinia and Cinque Terre pale in comparison. Apparently, it really is the simple things that kids enjoy.

What I didn't expect during this camping trip was a crash course in Dutch parenting. For all my bravado about going Dutch, I am still not completely sold on the idea of letting my toddler play unsupervised. I still feel I need to keep an eye on my child at all times. Isn't that what good parenting is all about? What if something happened to him? For the past three years, I have been sneaky about my hovering ways; I can helicopter unseen in our own home and garden.

Here, I don't have that freedom. If I want us to have dinner tonight, I need to let go so I can concentrate on the cooking. There's no way I can be in two places at once. Bram is busy trying to light the stove, so he can't cover for me. "Don't worry so much," he reassures me. Up until now, Bram has allowed me to lead our child-rearing. We live in his country, but we parent my way. "Let him play. He'll be fine. Besides, the nearest road is miles away."

Initially, I don't follow this advice. I creep after my toddler, trying my best to be inconspicuous. I find Julius in a small barn with a child-sized wheelbarrow loaded with toy cars. He is talking to the piglets, called Spek and Lap (Bacon and Rasher), showing off his newest treasures.

He picks up a toy and exclaims, "Dump truck!" The piglets grunt in excitement. He picks up another toy. "Fire truck!" Rinse and repeat. He is lost in his own world, surrounded by his new piglet friends. I exhale and let him be. I walk back to the tent, leaving Julius on his own, knowing that I will be less than fifteen steps away if he needs me. I am warming to the idea that children here can be even more free range than the chickens.

Bram spends the next two hours figuring out how to get the fire started and keep it going. I busy myself preparing the vegetables. It then takes another hour and a half to cook our modest one-pot meal of potatoes, corn, mushrooms, pieces of bacon and spring onions. This must be what slow living is all about. During this time, Julius happily wanders back and forth, every fifteen minutes or so.

I realize that camping ticks all the boxes of an essential element of Dutch parenting: allowing children to roam around freely in a relaxed setting. Nobody's worried that the other guests might be disturbed. Julius isn't the only child on the camp grounds. By six o'clock in the evening, all five tents are occupied by young families. We are sandwiched between a couple with four blond children and another with a three-year-old boy and a baby. The adults are focused on getting the fire going, and their kids run around the farm, laughing and shouting. No one seems to be too worried about it, or to mind.

On the Saturday evening, Niki and her husband Cees hold a pizza dinner for all the guests. Julius, not fond of crowds of strangers, is nowhere to be found. Neither is Bram, who is presumably following him around, trying to convince him to join the party. I apologize profusely to Niki, and notice that the other dozen or so toddlers and children are all happily playing together. Niki senses my discomfort and comments, "Parents often focus too much on the things that their children can't do, and not enough on what they can. Every child has their own unique talent." As I've mentioned before, the Dutch do have a knack for offering their opinion, whether it's been asked for or not.

"Thank you," I mutter, and we exchange knowing looks.

She adds, "Just let him be a three-year-old."

I turn away, touched. The Dutch may be direct, but they are also surprisingly kind and understanding. Here children are allowed to be children, rather than being expected to behave like miniature adults. My apology wasn't needed.

How Michele discovered the simple life

While Rina is still learning the joys of low-key parenting, I feel like I've gotten there with Ben and Ina. Birthdays are comfortably low-key, and we've become so relaxed about the timing that Ben is celebrating his tenth and eleventh birthdays in one go. We never got round to celebrating his tenth because he was hoping to have a snow party in the winter – only it failed to snow in Amsterdam last winter.

 Back home in London, my friends with children seem to have become infected by competitive birthday partying. When I was growing up, birthday parties consisted of a couple of school friends, a game of pass the parcel and the birthday child blowing out the candles on a cake. Expectations have escalated now. A friend back home took twenty-four children to a waterpark for her son's seventh birthday. Other friends have spent hundreds of pounds on entertainment, venue hire and catering. I've heard of people hiring expensive clowns, bouncy castles, magicians, puppet shows and even exotic-animal trainers.

I'm glad parents do things more simply in Amsterdam. Today, for his birthday, Ben has invited seven boys over. So far, all of them have been well-mannered and polite, talking and joking with each other; there's been no running around or screaming. About an hour ago they went off to the local swimming pool. My husband went along to pay the entrance charge, then left them there to come back on their own.

Now we are sitting around feeling a bit like spare parts. Though perhaps teenage parties will hold horrors in store for us, this is the most relaxed birthday party ever. Ben's birthday present from us is a modestly priced cell phone plan. It's a reward for not losing his pre-paid hand-me-down phone over a one-year period. He has proven that he can look after his property and that we can trust him not to run up excessive charges.

Last month, Ben attended a school friend's twelfth birthday party in which eight children went round to the girl's home and played with her new rabbit all afternoon. That's about as joyously low-key as it can get, right? I know that, sometimes, kids' parties can be hell, with a bunch of children running around out of control and a parent trying to figure out what on earth to do with them. Perhaps that's why people back in the UK have started throwing money at the problem.

With our eight-year-old, we haven't left the rough and tumble of the younger years behind entirely, but we did discover a way of making things easier. Ina, whose birthday is in February, had her last party half a year later so she could have it outdoors. Staying inside with a bunch of hectic boys is exhausting, as I know from her fifth-, sixth- and seventh-birthday parties, a couple of which I was foolish enough to undertake without my husband's help. (Dads are optional, remember?!) This year, we drove her and her boisterous friends out to the countryside for a game of football golf. Football golf is like mini-golf but with a football and on a course made of old bins and tires – a very inventive use of the flat strips of grass separated by irrigation channels (water features!) that make up the polder countryside. Cue three contented hours of running around in the mud and lots of laughs when balls landed in the ditch. All Mom and Dad had to do was keep the score.

Continuing the outdoor theme, another cute thing the Dutch tend to do for outdoor parties is simply to cordon off an area of the park by hanging streams of bunting from the trees. Then they'll lay down picnic rugs and light a portable barbecue in their little party corner. The same thing is done for adult parties sometimes, and in the summer the parks are often filled with people having mini celebrations.

The culture of simplicity

To understand why family holidays and children's birthday parties are so low-key, let's take a look at Dutch culture in general. Dutch frugality extends to other areas of life, too. One reason for Dutch houses looking modest but being large once you get inside is that during the Golden Age, in the seventeenth century, housing tax was calculated according to the width of the house, so tall, narrow houses that extend hugely at the back were constructed. Think of Anne Frank's annex: an entire living space hidden behind a small-looking house. Windows in Dutch houses are huge, letting in as much light as possible to offset the gloom of cloudy skies, and curtains are perennially open, without net curtains, to show that you have no riches to hide (and that your house is tidy and spotless).

In *Moet kunnen* (Must be possible), Herman Pleij typifies the Dutch as *doodgewone mensen* (dead-normal people).[3] There is a strong urge to keep everyone on the same level. Putting celebrities on a pedestal is unheard of, and there are few statues of famous aristocrats or politicians. (The people that are remembered in this way are usually working-class heroes like the popular singer André Hazes or the seventeenth-century admiral Michiel de Ruyter, who fought the English and the French at sea, or the writer Multatuli, who exposed the injustices of colonial rule in the Dutch East Indies.) Even sports

Dutch birthday-party ideas

Due to popular request, Ina twice had a cardboard box party. What you need: cardboard boxes (at least one per child), a roll of silver foil, stickers, pens, crepe paper. Leave them to it and see what they come up with. (Ina's friends made spaceships.)

And Ben had two drawing-table parties. What you need: a roll of brown packing paper from a stationery store (cover your dinner table with it and tape it down), pencils, pens, crayons, stickers. Again, leave them to it!

Another idea, as long as it snows, is a snow party. Obviously, this may have to be arranged on very short notice (it doesn't matter when your child's birthday falls). The children make Minecraft-style snow blocks and build whatever they like.

Ina's friend Madelief recently had a plastic bag party. What you need: strong plastic bags, scissors, tape. The children cut the plastic bags into strips, then weave them into mats. The mats are then ironed on a low heat (some parental involvement required here) and the resulting sheets cut and sewn to make wallets and pencil cases.

Another idea is to have a sports day party. We took a length of rope, some potato sacks and chalk to the park. I chalked a start and finish line on the path for a race. We held a tug-o'-war, which proved incredibly popular, and a sack race. You can also play a good Dutch party game called *koekje-hap*. String up pieces of gingerbread cake between two trees. The children have to hold their hands behind their back and try to bite some off.

Lastly, someone in the Netherlands has invented the novel art of tea-bag-wrapper folding, also known as miniature kaleidoscopic origami. Since they don't like anything to go to waste, some Dutch people empty and save the tea bag paper sachets and make artwork from them. Look it up on YouTube! Anyway, it's one idea for a creative party. Tip: A rule of thumb in Holland is to invite as many children as your child's age, so seven children to a seven-year-old's party. (Teachers encourage parents and children not to hand out the invitations in class but before or after school, to avoid anyone feeling left out.)

personalities are referred to by their first names, and their normalcy is celebrated. "In particular, their failings and other dramatic vicissitudes in their life are widely reported," Pleij reports.

Even in medieval times, the Dutch liked to be inconspicuous. Medieval traders from the Low Countries would dress in plain black clothing, while Italians would swan around in gold brocade. In the Netherlands, this had commercial advantages and led to less envy and thus better working relationships. Culturally, it's not done to be flash with your cash. Pleij encapsulates the Dutch mentality in a stream of Dutch catchwords and phrases: "'simplicity, thrift, self-sufficiency,' 'actions not words,' straightforwardness, 'just act normal,' 'don't get any ideas,' 'tomorrow's another day,' diversification, 'long live the nuclear family'; and the reduction of leaders into 'fathers of the national household.'"[4]

Middle-class parenting in the Netherlands shares the same egalitarian, communal tendency, and that is one of its strengths. There's no attempting to outdo the Joneses – or, in the case of the Dutch, the Heinekens – in terms of expensive birthday presents or fancy children's clothes. There's a silent pact that presents for your children's friend's birthdays should cost no more than ten euros (roughly equivalent to ten dollars). And the traditions of a Dutch Christmas run counter to the rampant consumerism of the US and UK model. For

December 5, the eve of St. Nicholas' name day, children draw lots at school to see which of their classmates they will be making a present for – making, not buying. Then they carefully craft a *surprise* (pronounced *sur-preez*), typically a cardboard or papier mâché model related to the recipient's favorite hobby. Ina received a giant cardboard electric guitar last year, for example (it's still taking up half her bedroom). A small gift worth exactly 3.50 euros (about 3.75 dollars) is hidden inside the *surprise*, and the recipient also receives a rhyming poem praising their strengths and gently teasing them about their weaknesses. Families celebrate St. Nicholas in a similar fashion – with homemade presents accompanied by funny doggerel poems – again, lots are drawn to determine who buys for whom. Food is kept simple, so there is no massive turkey roast but something easy to prepare like a stew or soup, followed by pastries and sweets, typically, an almond pastry roll and letters made out of chocolate.

Children growing up in the Netherlands are used to having secondhand toys. Each year on King's Day in April, as part of the *vrijmarkt* (the unregulated street market), the Vondelpark in Amsterdam is transformed into a massive open-air children's market, and this is replicated in villages and towns all around the country. The children sell their old clothes and toys and buy new ones with the proceeds. It's the best example of recycling I've seen and an excellent way to teach children about pricing, bartering and money management. Other forms of social sharing are also big here. Amsterdam Noord boasts the largest flea market in Europe, and Facebook groups like Amsterdam Yard Sale and Family Market offer low-priced children's toys and clothes. There is no shame in being seen using or wearing somebody else's castoffs. It just makes sense, and it's good for the environment, to boot.

Anja from my book club has two boys and lives in an attractively decorated house on a new housing development nearby. She happily confesses to being addicted to buying secondhand stuff online. She hopes that in this way her sons will learn "respect and care for their environment, both in terms of nature and their direct surroundings." She tells me she thinks "happiness, beauty and peace all come from a slower pace of life." It's better not to be swept along with the consumerist tide. "And what's more, buying secondhand stuff is great fun!"

Madea, her twins now teenagers, is also a big advocate of the simple life. She's always bought her children secondhand clothes, and she grew up wearing them, too. Her children aren't particularly materialistic and she sees nothing like the rampant consumerism here that she has experienced when visiting her brother in the US. As for vacations: "We go on city trips as a family but we also go camping," she tells me. "I think it represents the ultimate freedom for children. I went camping myself when I was a child and strongly associate it with a feeling of happiness."

While many American and British kids are being brought up surrounded by the spoils of a booming consumer economy and demand the latest toys and fashions, Dutch kids are playing outdoors in nearly new clothes on secondhand roller skates. One of the things we know about happiness is that people are happier in countries where there is less social inequality. In *The Spirit Level: Why Equality Is Better for Everyone*, Richard Wilkinson and Kate Pickett write, "Like health, how happy people are rises in the early stages of economic growth and then levels off."[5] The authors go on to build an argument that it is inequality, not poverty, that has the greatest negative effect on well-being. Consumerism may, for many people, be inextricably linked with the building of their identity, but what mainly drives it is *status competition*: Some think that "second-class goods make us look like second-class people." Only new will do. Hence the obsession with box-fresh sneakers and the tendency to discard clothing as soon as there are minor traces of wear.

Wilkinson and Pickett explain that many issues related to inequality arise in response to status anxiety, and that inequality causes all kinds of problems for children:

These include juvenile conflict, poor peer relationships and educational performance at school, childhood obesity, infant mortality and teenage pregnancy. Problems such as these are likely to reflect the way the stresses of a more unequal society – of low social status – have penetrated family life and relationships. Inequality is associated with less good outcomes because it leads to a deterioration in the quality of relationships.[6]

While inequality has risen dramatically over the last few decades in most developed countries, with the gap between rich and poor becoming ever more impossible to breach, the Netherlands is unique in bucking the trend. Here, levels of inequality have not increased. Some of the reasons, I am sure, are Holland's love of frugality, its aversion to ostentation, and its flat social hierarchy and, of course, the high taxes. The Dutch opt for time, not money, and practicality over luxury goods. What Dutch children grow accustomed to in childhood sets them up for life: they are pragmatic and confident, unhampered by anxieties about status.

10

Happy Parents Have Happy Kids

In which Rina discovers a life-work balance

I keep coming to the same conclusion: Dutch mothers are not like me. Or, more accurately, I am not like them. I still struggle to evoke the calm, confident and self-assured aura they radiate as they juggle the demands of family and career, and at the same time maintain their own identity outside of motherhood.

In the *New York Times* article "Why Dutch Women Don't Get Depressed," Dutch psychologist Ellen de Bruin is quoted as claiming that while it isn't true that Dutch women *can't* become depressed, women in the Netherlands are a whole lot happier than their counterparts in the rest of the world.[1] After meticulous research and in-depth interviews with Dutch women from different backgrounds, de Bruin contends that the underlying secrets of their happiness are the personal freedoms they enjoy and a good work-life balance. Part of this is feeling free to work part-time, or not at all.

And among these Dutch women are of course Dutch mothers. If Dutch kids are the happiest kids in the world, then surely their moms deserve recognition. What are the personal freedoms that these Dutch moms have that other moms, especially in the US and Britain, have yet to discover? What can we learn from them? They have a similar child-centered approach to parenting, yet they don't seem to carry the same kind of baggage as moms where we come from.

My mother, like most American moms, followed an unspoken and understood pursuit of perfect parenting, Martha Stewart–style: Mothers were indentured servants to their kitchen, their work, their children and their husbands – and, most often, they did it alone. There was a lot of dignity and pride when it came to being a supermom. The more sacrifices you made – including neglecting to look after or take any time for yourself – the better you were at being a mom.

It's also become a common American practice to measure ourselves against other moms. We view the perceived successes and failures of other women's children and ours as a direct reflection of our parenting styles. What initially started as a sincere drive – wanting the best for our children – morphed into a hungry desire: wanting our children to be the best.

I want a different reality for my children. And I'm convinced I have found it in this tiny corner of Western Europe. The ideal of a perfect mom isn't emphasized so much over here. I am often admonished by my mother-in-law, Marcia, because she's afraid I'm doing too much. Even though she's supportive of me writing this book, she doesn't approve of the fact that I started writing it while I was heavily pregnant, and am writing it now, while taking care of a newborn and a toddler. My and Bram's entrepreneurial lifestyle – with all the risk, the irregular, long hours and the fact that we are always on call – stresses her out. It's a long way off the Dutch model, where work contracts are permanent, working part-time is more than acceptable and holidays are guaranteed. She thinks we should take it easy. "Don't forget to make time for yourself," she warns us regularly. "You also need time to rest and recover. Don't forget about yourselves."

Dutch moms have redefined the meaning of "having it all." They have plenty of time for their children; they can choose to stay at home, work part-time or full-time, according to their own preference, without financial or social pressure. There doesn't seem to be any form of competition among moms to be the perfect mother.

Michele and I are convinced that the peer pressure mothers feel elsewhere in the developed world comes largely from a sense of guilt. Where we come from, there are pressures to be both a homemaker and a working mother. Stay-at-home moms feel guilty about not working and compensate by being domestic mother goddesses. Working moms feel guilty about not being available to their kids all the time and compensate by baking cookies for tomorrow's bake sale at midnight and cobbling together a Halloween costume after a full, stressful day in the office. It's a lose-lose situation.[2]

Dig a bit deeper, and it's the bootstrap mentality in the Anglophone world that incites this guilt, anxiety and judgement. According to research from the University of Texas, when comparing the happiness of parents and non-parents in twenty-two European and English-speaking countries, researchers came to one resounding conclusion:

> The negative effects of parenthood on happiness were *entirely* explained by the presence or absence of social policies allowing parents to better combine paid work with family obligations. And this was true for both mothers and fathers. Countries with the better family policy "packages" had no happiness gap between parents and non-parents.[3]

"I feel blessed that I have really managed to find a balance. I work three days a week and, if we have to go to the *consultatiebureau*, it's no problem if I'm a little late to work," Eva Brouwer, a TV presenter for RTV Utrecht, tells me. "When Rijck celebrated his first birthday on a Monday, my husband and I went to the crèche together. We sang songs, and Rijck had his little party hat on. I took loads of pictures. And although it made me late for work, my colleagues and boss fully understood that I wanted to be there for this special moment and shared my enthusiasm."

Eva is the first friend I made in Holland, and she's over at my house for lunch. I take the opportunity to pick her brains.

"Do you think that Dutch moms are under much less pressure to have it all, compared to American moms?" I ask.

"Actually, since becoming a mom, I have a bigger drive to make something of my career. I work more efficiently because I also want to be with my family," Eva tells me. "I think the opportunity to work part-time is a wonderful way to balance private time and a career. It's great that there is no taboo about that."

"What also helps is that we are allowed to be very open and honest in our culture. Of course, people in the Netherlands are keeping up appearances, too, but I think it's easier here to be frank about the questions and doubts you may have about parenting."

My near-daily Facebook Messenger conversations with my friends in the US tell me that the drive to be a perfect mother there is as strong as ever. The first mom-friend that comes to mind is Tara Wood, a writer. She has a brood of seven and is married to a "hot guy" (her words) and living in Augusta, Georgia.

I ask her about stress. "I think it *can* be stressful to be an American mom, yes. I'd imagine that most moms, no matter where they live, are stressed, but I do think that American moms tend to be more competitive, judgmental and tightly wound, which probably adds to feelings of anxiety, angst and self-doubt. After nearly fifteen years of parenting, it is only in the past five years that I've felt comfortable with my own thoughts and decisions as a mother. It took a long time, but I now know that the way I am and how I parent are really none of their business. And, on my part, I sincerely try not to judge parenting styles and choices that may be different from my own. There is no one way to be a good mother."

Facebook's chief operative officer, Sheryl Sandberg, who coined the term "lean in" – as in, "a lean-in mother can have it all" – created an internet sensation when, in her 2011 Barnard College commencement address in New York, she said, "The most important career decision you're going to make is whether or not you have a life partner and who that partner is."

I wholeheartedly agree with Sandberg on the partner issue – that he needs to believe in equal roles. She could have added that you should seriously consider marrying a Dutch guy. Dutch men don't have a reputation for being romantic, like the French, or great in bed, like the Italians. Here, the courtship model works both ways – it's more than OK for women to ask men out. Once you get past the initial awkward phase of having to pay for your share of the meal on the first date (also known as "going Dutch," of course), you'll realize that Dutch men are the best-kept European secret. For one thing, they're genuinely interested in what you have to say: Being able to speak your mind is a trait that is highly valued in both men and women.

In Holland, the division of labor between men and women, moms and dads, has evolved radically. Another thing Dutch men are known for, like the Scandinavians, is excelling in the things that can make a big difference to a family's overall happiness: pulling their weight at home and sharing parenting responsibilities equally. Though things aren't perfect yet – Dutch women are still bearing more of the childcare and household responsibilities – it is evident that times are changing. According to recent statistics from the Netherlands Central Statistics Bureau, men are doing more cooking and cleaning, and the time women spend on such activities is decreasing.

The culture of part-time work is another reason why everyone is much happier over here. The Dutch have the shortest average working hours of any OECD country and work the fewest hours per week of any country in the EU. Nearly half of the Dutch adult population (again, by far the highest percentage in the EU), works part-time, with 26.8 percent of men working less than the maximum thirty-six hours a week and 75 percent of women working part-time – and this is across all sectors, from unskilled laborers to professionals.[4]

Compare this to the UK, where 25 percent of the population works part-time (13 percent of men, and 43 percent of women). In the US, the percentage is even lower: 18.9 percent (12.6 percent of men, and 25.8 percent of women). In Holland, part-time work has become the norm: For many Dutch fathers, it is as important to share childcare and household chores as it is to pursue their career. They understand the importance of having a more active role at home and are lucky to have employers who understand and support this.

The role of dads in the development and well-being of children is now recognized by researchers and medical professionals; there is plenty of compelling evidence in the scientific literature. The HBSC studies that formed the basis of UNICEF's report on child well-being suggests that Dutch children's relationships with their fathers have improved incrementally in step with the increased time dads spend caring for their children.

When the full-time working week was reduced to thirty-six hours in the Netherlands to combat unemployment, the government compensated those who had been working a forty-hour, nine-to-five week by giving them extra vacation of half a day a week, or one day a fortnight. This time off is frequently used by fathers as their *Papadag*. Taking a "Daddy day" is becoming the norm, as more and more Dutch fathers see the benefit of spending time with their kids at least once a week.[5] (Some Dutch parents are offended by the word *Papadag*, as it implies more of a babysitting role for fathers rather than equitable shared parenting responsibilities 24-7. The proposed alternative is *kinderdag*, but even then there is no consensus to the word.)

Curious to know more about *Papadag*, I ask a close friend of mine, Mathijs, about it. "*Papadag* is pretty common, especially within the public and government sectors here. It was an easy choice for me to work four days a week. I appreciate the extra time I get to spend with my daughter alone and, while she's napping or playing with a friend, I can work a bit, too, checking email and doing some short-attention work," he says.

"I read some time ago that the male influence is important for a kid, especially when there's a lot of female teachers at school. Let the dad be the dad. That means going outdoors, doing physical stuff with her, wrestling and fighting a bit. For example, today, Friday, I was looking after her after school. She had a friend with her, and I took them into town on my bike. Got them outside, to catch some UV light and fresh air in these dark November days. We ran through the shopping mall, made a few turns round a revolving door, cracked jokes, and then I bought them each a chocolate Sinterklaas [St. Nicholas].

"Afterwards, when her friend had gone home, we went out again for some football in front of our house. I also organized a cycling competition with the boy next door. A bit of physical stuff, good for her and fun for me as well!"

In my family, we follow a more traditional model, with me working part-time at home as a freelance writer and my husband working full-time. Yet Bram, too, does his share of *Papadag*, only he spends time with them on weekends rather than during the working week. He's in charge of the week's grocery shopping, taking our three-year-old with him, and does all the weekend cleaning, laundry and vacuuming, after which he'll take Julius to the zoo or the pool. When our baby is a little older, he'll take over with him, too. For me, it's my time to catch up, when Matteo is sleeping, on finishing writing assignments, blog posts and other projects.

In a culture where one's job is inextricably linked to one's identity, American dads who *lean out* can face isolation and stigma. Many men of my generation aspire to be hands-on fathers who change diapers, cook dinner and do the laundry. But the sad reality is that for many who start out with these lofty, progressive ideals, the pressures at work, in the long run, make it impossible.

In America, parenting is seen as your problem: a private rather than a communal concern. You've taken the decision to have children, that's your choice – deal with it. In the Netherlands, however, it's something for which the whole society takes responsibility. Dutch parents often have a rich support network consisting of grandparents, siblings and neighbors who can be counted on to keep an eye on the children. The ideal child-care structure consists of both parents working part-time, and the family getting additional help from both sets of grandparents, neighbors and the local crèche, or from "guest parents" – certified babysitters who look after the children in their own home. It's the modern-day village.

Can women really have fulfilling part-time work and also have time to enjoy motherhood? Is there really such a thing as a work-life balance even for the most ambitious of women?

To get a better understanding of this, I invite Doortje, a doctor who also lives in Doorn, over for coffee. Doortje and her husband are living the ideal Dutch model of both working part-time; Doortje three days a week, and her husband, a notary, four. They have three kids, and a dog, too.

"What inspired you to go part-time?" I ask Doortje.

"It was never a question for me *not* to work part-time. When I finished my doctor's degree and I was thinking about what I was going to do, I wanted a job that would also give me time for a family," she explains. "So I decided to be a general practitioner – a job that allows for that flexibility: Since having children, I now work three days a week. Although, if you count up all the hours I work, it adds up to more than a full-time job," Doortje is quick to add.

"How many hours is it?"

"I start work at a quarter to eight, and then, most days, I get home between half past six and half past seven. So, that's about a ten- to eleven-hour day," says Doortje. "Then, after I put the kids to bed I often have to go back to my computer and work. And I also have meetings on other days, and I'm often on call on the weekends. But what I really like is that I can do it around my family life and have time for myself. On Mondays and Wednesdays, my days at home, I am able to go to the gym and have coffee with friends. And when the kids are at home, I spend time with them. Because I want to be there for them."

"You know, it's funny that you ask me how I manage to have a work-life balance," laughs Doortje. "My friend Suzanne texted me last night asking me the same thing. She thinks I'm a supermom. Want to see the text that I sent her in return?"

Of course I did. Holding her phone in front of me, I read, "Mine are tucked up at last, after a lot of screaming at them that they have to stay in their beds, that Papa and Mama have still got a lot of work to do and we still need to tidy the kitchen, write the email about the earrings for Mijntje's Madonna act, and draw the color-in umbrellas for Emmy's birthday party. And Papa hasn't emptied the bloody bins yet. So if you see me cycling past you tomorrow with an exhausted look on my face, you'll know why."

For a mother like Doortje, modern life still poses challenges and stresses that parents around the world can relate to. However, thanks to the part-time work culture, she is still able to have time for herself. And that makes all the difference for a happier mom.

In which Michele learns to take it easy

When I started work in the Netherlands, I continued at the frantic pace I'd picked up in London. There was a lot to be done; efficiency and speed were crucial. I truly believed my particular skill set would be appreciated. As far as I was concerned, you work until the job is done, even if that involves unpaid overtime. Your work defines your identity, and being good at it is at the foundation of your self-worth.

I was the very model of the ideal worker. But there was a surprise in store for me.

By that time, Benjamin was a year old and enjoying his time at the local crèche. My modest earnings qualified us for a government subsidy, so we got a chunk of the costs back. He'd taken to it from day one. He was a sunny-natured, sociable baby who always perked up in company. I had no scruples about leaving him there. He was happy. What's more, the Dutch attitude to crèches is more relaxed than in the UK. While parents in English-speaking countries might worry about the psychological effects of leaving babies and young children in an institutional environment all day, Dutch parents see crèches as places where children learn to play with other children. It is good for their social development. And picking up germs along the way helps them develop a robust immune system.

In Germany, I may well have been called a *Rabenmutter* (a "raven mother"; the birds are known for neglecting their young), but in the Netherlands there is no shame in working rather than being a stay-at-home mom. Both are considered equally valid options, as is a combination of the two, it seems. Having only the English full-time model in my cultural background, and since all the jobs I found were part-time, I ended up taking on three different publishing jobs. Back then, I couldn't understand why everything I was offered was for just one or two days a week. I assumed that it was cheaper to hire people that way. Later, I found out that part-time work is simply the norm here. The Dutch pride themselves on being "the part-time work champions of Europe," as Rina has explained. It's seen as something that allows you a better work-life balance, even if you don't have children. Mothers and fathers often opt for part-time work so they can spend more time with their children. It doesn't affect their social status and they aren't stigmatized or treated as less valuable at the office. In the US and the UK, all the emphasis is on spending "quality time" with your children, since time is in short supply. In the Netherlands, on the other hand, there's less emphasis on making your time with your kids extra special, because you have a lot more time to spend with them. Rina and I each had a lightbulb moment about that.

My former colleague Madea, who works as a project manager, tells me that both she and her husband opted to work part-time when their twins were born and to share the childcare equally: "We consciously chose less income in exchange for more time with our children." She feels there is still some inequality: Men still earn more, as a rule, and women still do more of the childcare. "I don't like the word *Papadag*," she tells me. "It suggests that Mama is responsible the rest of the time! But then again, women *enjoy* being with their children. I feel it, too – there's something very natural about spending time with your child, so some women don't mind taking on more of the responsibility."

Indeed, many Dutch women see spending time with their children rather than working as a benefit, a luxury. Betty, our babysitter, for example, was a stay-at-home mom until her kids left home. She didn't at all feel her social status was reduced by this and felt quite equal to her husband. "I was busy with my children and didn't have time for anything other than my voluntary work as a breastfeeding advisor. I was following my mother's example. She'd loved being a mother and doing that exclusively, and I did, too."

When Rina and I met up with Els Kloek, a leading historian who focuses on women's issues, we talked about some of this. We put it to her that, to us at least, identity seems less tied up in work in Amsterdam than in London or San Francisco. It's considered normal to work part-time or not at all; it's not a loss of face.

"Exactly!" she exclaimed. "Because of a strong tradition of homeliness and *gezelligheid*, Dutch women feel not working is a privilege. At work, you have to work long days, you have to obey a boss. At home, you are the only boss, your own boss. That's what some feminists tend to forget."

Els' study of the Dutch housewife throughout the ages, *Vrouw des Huizes* (Lady of the house), presents an image of the Dutch woman as incredibly strong and in control of her life, despite not always having had the same political rights as her husband. Els delves into the historical caricature of the Dutch housewife as "bossy, enterprising, thrifty and incredibly neat and tidy." It's clear to us why Dutch women don't get hung up on male-imposed ideals of what a woman should be. There's no attempt to squeeze back into pre-pregnancy jeans postpartum; it's just not a priority. And the Dutch homemaker makes her home nice for herself, not to please her husband.

"She is most clearly revealed in everything she is not: She isn't a slave or a skivvy [housemaid], she isn't a *femme fatale* and she isn't the queen of the kitchen," Els writes in her introduction, and continues:

> The reputation of a woman from the Netherlands mainly revolves around her dominant position both in the home and in the marriage. She may be less well dressed than a *française* and less obedient than a German woman, she might not organize receptions as well as an English lady, but she is much more than the equal of her husband. She stands alongside, if not above, her husband.[6]

Els argues that it would be wrong to consider what a "housewife" does as a profession. A housewife's work exists outside the economy; paying her a wage would make her her husband's wage slave, creating inequality. Being a housewife is not a job as much as a position in society. "In the Dutch context, the housewife was usually exempt from work; being a housewife was a luxury: As soon as people could afford it, the woman would quit paid work and take care of the family, while the man brought home the wages."[7] Els suggests that, historically, the Dutch housewife was always the boss of the household. She wouldn't spend hours in the kitchen but enjoyed keeping her home neat and clean. She wasn't erudite and she didn't run intellectual salons, but she was good at arithmetic and ran the household accounts. There are plenty of historical examples of widows running their late husband's companies, or even taking up arms. And visitors from abroad were constantly amazed that Dutch women seemed to wear the trousers in the home.

Els recommends that we contact Roos Wouters for a modern-day take on Dutch women's liberation. Roos describes herself as a political scientist and social entrepreneur. She is the author of *Fuck! Ik ben een feminist* (Fuck! I'm a feminist) and gives talks and runs workshops on reducing stress at work. She has also done a lot of work to promote the New Way of Working. This movement has helped companies provide greater flexibility for working parents, allowing more work to be done from home and allowing employees to work the hours they choose. We meet up with Roos in the Amsterdam central library, a lovely modern building next to the train station, flooded with light.

Roos, who has two children aged eleven and fifteen, begins by explaining her own experiences as a part-time mother. Her partner was working full-time and she was working three days a week at a TV company and feeling the stress of combining work and childcare. One day, when she was on a tight deadline, she forgot that her father was unable to pick up her son from school, so didn't make alternative arrangements. Luckily, a fellow mom was able to step in and take the child to her house, but receiving that shaming phone call was a pivotal moment in Roos' life. She felt there was something wrong with the common Dutch model of a working father and a mother who worked part-time. It just didn't work for an ambitious woman like her.

Journalist Brigid Schulte comes to the same conclusion in her book *Overwhelmed: How to Work, Love and Play when No One Has the Time*. In her study of the helter-skelter modern lifestyle, which makes a cult of hectic busyness, she mentions the older Dutch model with its full-time fathers and part-time mothers. Although this might sound ideal, she warns that part-time work can create "role overload," and that constantly switching from one role to the other adds to the feeling of time pressure.[8] Working mothers are the most susceptible to this, because they automatically take on more responsibility for the home and multitask, whereas fathers tend to focus on work.

There seems to be something else contributing to stress in mothers, even in the Netherlands, whether they work part-time or not. New research by the Dutch Social Policy Unit has shown that while men and women in the Netherlands often have equal amounts of free time, women don't experience their free time as "free" because they are always preoccupied with making sure their partners and children are happy or that the house is tidy. The researchers call this "emotion work."[9] It seems us mothers make things harder for ourselves, even when the culture is conspiring to help us.[10]

Roos started lobbying for more flexibility at work for women and men in the Netherlands and more opportunity to work from home, whether you work full- or part-time. She feels things have moved along a great deal over the last decade. "The constrictive division of labor between the two parents used to be a private problem, something to be fixed around the kitchen table, not something to bother your employer about. Now, things have changed." She feels that the New Way of Working really has improved the working climate and given parents more room to maneuver. "We used to look to the Swedish as role models; now, they are coming here to see how we are doing things," she adds proudly. "These days, work stress is something that can be openly discussed. It's everyone's problem."

As we draw the interview to a close, I mention to Roos that both of us have now found the ultimate type of New Working – by becoming freelancers. She agrees that, partly due to the financial crisis and the fact that companies are downscaling, more and more people are working freelance. It suits us; better than your boss giving you increased flexibility at work is to have no boss at all.

Stress

As the French philosopher Descartes, who spent much of his adult life in the Netherlands, is reported to have said, "God created the world, but the Dutch created Holland." He was referring to the way the Dutch have battled to reclaim their land from the encroaching sea, but his words can also be applied to other ways in which they have fought to establish their own social principles. The Dutch are actively and consciously resistant to social hierarchies. Politicians do their best to manage the gap between the rich and poor with fiscal instruments such as taxation (which funds the welfare state and allows for free schooling). But it's not just the politicians doing the social engineering, it comes from the people themselves. Individual aspirations don't often run to being the richest (or "the best"). As the popular Dutch saying goes, "Don't stick your head up above the cornfield or it'll be mowed off." It makes working in Holland rather fascinating for a foreigner.

By the time I'd been here a year, I was employed by a poetry festival and two publishing companies who were, officially, in competition with each other, but that didn't seem to bother either of them. The atmosphere was relaxed, the office spaces were gorgeous, in stylish buildings, slightly run down but with the kind of charming genteel shabbiness you might have seen in British publishing thirty years ago. The only downside was the lengthy meetings. People were so relaxed they would invariably descend into chit-chat. There was no sense of time pressure at all. Everyone around the table would be expected to offer their opinion on the matter at hand and rarely were any decisions made. Witness the aforementioned polder model in action.

After a couple of months at one company, my boss took me aside and said, "Could you slow down a little? You're unsettling your colleagues. Things are getting out of balance." An English friend who also moved here told me she had the same experience working in a totally different sector. "I can't believe it – my boss told me not to work so hard!" she exclaimed. Colin White and Laurie Boucke's humorous study of life in the Netherlands, *The UnDutchables*, warns that expats will be frustrated by their colleagues' lack of effort; here, work is the interruption of coffee breaks, they joke, with colleagues' birthdays taking top priority.[11]

Yet, strangely enough, the Dutch themselves seem to believe they work particularly hard; they are very proud of their Calvinist work ethic. "*Arbeid adelt*," they say: "There is nobility in labor." In my opinion, they didn't seem to work anywhere near as hard as my colleagues in the UK did. Yet, to my surprise, the OECD stats on productivity show that, when the Dutch work, they get a lot done. Productivity levels are significantly higher than those in the UK.[12] The Dutch believe in working hard and playing hard. "*Na gedane arbeid is goed rusten*" is another popular saying: "After work is done, repose is sweet." So there's no reason not to take time out to enjoy life. When the sun shines, which it tends not to do very much here, the café terraces fill up with office workers taking an unofficial yet perfectly acceptable spontaneous break. Carpe diem![13]

Despite my boss's request, I didn't slow down. I didn't know how to; I was too British. I continued to juggle jobs and work as hard and conscientiously as I could. Ben went to the crèche four days a week and spent the fifth day with his grandmother. But when Ina was born, I found myself dealing with a different kind of child; she was not as easy to leave while I went to work. She seemed to hate being at the crèche. She hated crowds, she hated strangers, she hated being anywhere other than clasped tight to my chest.

Back in 2007, when she was born, freelancers didn't get maternity pay here, though, Sod's law, a year later it was introduced. So, during my eight months at home with Ina, my financial solution was to translate a Dutch novel. After that, I went back to just one of my jobs, which had expanded to four days a week. (I translated books freelance on the fifth day – no rest for the compulsive worker.) It was the one company I had worked for where they actively encouraged me to increase my hours. At the same time, they were implementing Roos' New Way of Working, so there was a good degree of flexibility. I was able to work from home at least one day a week and fit things around the kids. They were difficult years – what I call "the tunnel" of child-rearing, when the combination of a baby and a toddler is simply exhausting. Still, it was doable with understanding employers, a local crèche and a lovely retired neighbor who became a kind of third grandmother.

When, a couple of years later, the stress of a merger at the company reared its ugly head, I found myself lying awake most nights worrying about how things would work out. I went to see the HR manager. She realized that I was doing myself no favors and sent me to see a haptonomist. During working hours, of course.

I'd heard haptonomy mentioned only in connection with the Dutch national football team, as some kind of New Age therapy used to help the footballers bond with each other, to relax and avoid injuries. Some even attributed Oranje's success in 1988, when they won the European Championship, to their haptonomist, Ted Troost. I was very suspicious of it, to say the least. Somehow, the name carried a whiff of scary weird stuff like Scientology.

In a small office near the main train station, in a room containing a massage bed and very little else, I was rapidly diagnosed as an anxious intellectual who needed to stop overthinking life. Whatever I did, the therapist said, I was not allowed to look up haptonomy online, or read any books about it, during the course of my therapy. I didn't, and I haven't done since. It was an odd kind of therapy, part talking, part healing and massage. This is what I was asked to do:

- Reconnect with my body and its needs
- Be more pushy
- Keep things in perspective
- Not overthink stuff

- Stand up for myself more
- Learn to say no

Basically, I had to become more like a self-confident Dutch woman! The message of haptonomy is that your physical and mental health are more important than your work. It's advice many of my English friends could take to heart.

The Dutch have an excellent handle on that elusive life-work balance we hear so much about. OECD statistics published in their Better Life Index place the Netherlands as second only to Denmark, with the UK in twenty-second place, and the US twenty-eighth out of the thirty-four advanced nations surveyed.[14] This approach to life was apparent in the working environment, where, even when I was working my hardest, I was never expected to stay late. In the beginning, I was frequently the last one switching off the lights, whereas in London, 7:00 PM was seen as a normal time to go home. Here, there was always a mass exodus at five. Parents would hurry off to collect their kids, and the childless would go and hang out in bars or head off to the gym. As I mentioned before, being a high flyer is not something anyone particularly wants to be in Holland. Office face time, hanging around the office or staying late to make sure others see that you are there, is not normal behavior here. As a working mother, the advantages were obvious. There was no stress about getting back in time to pick up my children from the crèche. Sure, I had lots of reading to do; I was in publishing. But I could do that when the children were in bed.

I remember comparing my work day – in which I'd drop off the kids ten minutes from my house by bike, then cycle on to work a further twenty minutes away, and work from nine to just five – to that of my friend Helen in London at the time. She had a forty-five minute train commute to the office from her house in Surrey to the city. Her daughter was at a nursery close to her home, but my friend lived in constant anxiety because she felt that she was too far away should anything happen to her child. Her husband was doing the drop-off in the morning so she could get to work on time. It was a strained existence, and one I've heard recounted by many people. Working mothers in Britain are expected to work just as long hours as they did before they had children. As I saw it from my cozy Amsterdam nest, becoming a mother wasn't the problem; the real problem was the culture of overwork in the UK and the continuing belief that work defines your identity.

11

It's All about the *Hagelslag*

In which Rina explains the Dutch attitude to meals

Lazy Sundays are an absolute must in our household. In any case, most places are closed, or open only in the afternoon – if you're lucky. Bram will be busy in the kitchen, preparing an elaborate breakfast, and I'll be on the couch in the living room, breastfeeding Matteo and planning our afternoon nature walk. Julius will be in his room, playing on his own with his Duplo.

Today, the morning sunshine and crisp fall air outside have put us in a good mood. Bram is making *wentelteefjes*, the Dutch version of French toast (see recipe on page 175), which he serves with goat cheese and strawberries, mango and blueberries. I'm looking up local trails on which to hunt for fly agaric, those elusive red mushrooms with white dots on them. Until I moved to the Netherlands, I thought that these red mushrooms belonged in the fantasy world of *Super Mario Brothers*, in fairy tales, or with garden gnomes. It turns out they grow plentifully here, and are known for their toxicity and hallucinogenic properties. We're on a mission simply to admire these beauties from a distance.

"My love, take a look at this," cries out Bram from the kitchen-dining area.

I turn my head toward the table. Julius is sitting in his high chair, an infectious grin on his face. Our three-year-old has helped himself to breakfast. In front of him is a piece of bread piled high with unsalted butter and *hagelslag* – chocolate sprinkles.

"No wonder Dutch kids are the happiest kids in the world," I think to myself. "Who wouldn't be happy if they could have chocolate first thing every morning?"

I can already hear gasps of disapproval and disdain from the perfect moms of the internet. Chocolate for breakfast? You wouldn't think that starting the morning with a sugar rush would be a brilliant idea. And he's created a horrible mess. Butter is smeared all over his high chair, as well as his face and hands, and there are chocolate sprinkles all over the floor.

My husband and I look at each other. Shall we reprimand him? Instead, we burst out laughing and count it as another sanctimommy fail. Oblivious, Julius starts gobbling his *hagelslag* sandwich, and my husband snaps a picture of his happy face.

Breakfast of champions

So is there something special about eating *hagelslag* for breakfast? Is that really what makes Dutch children so happy? Judging by the reactions of American kids on a fascinating Buzzfeed video inviting them to try traditional breakfasts from around the world, it was clear that this Dutch breakfast had won their hearts. What kid wouldn't want to eat breakfast every morning if chocolate was on the menu? But kids in other countries also eat sugar-laden foods, often in the form of cereal – Coco

Pops spring to mind. No, I think it's more about the fact that the Dutch eat breakfast as a family.

According to the 2013 UNICEF report – the one that suggested that Dutch kids were the happiest in the world – 85 percent of the Dutch children aged eleven, thirteen and fifteen surveyed ate breakfast every day. Sitting down to eat around the table as a family, before school and the working day, is a routine that underpins Dutch family life. In no other country do families eat breakfast together as regularly as they do in the Netherlands. I'm aware that, in American and British families, breakfast is a meal that's often skipped altogether, in the rush to get out of the house on time.

What the Dutch seem to understand is the importance of eating regular meals, starting with the meal that breaks the nighttime fast. There's an abundance of research that points out the benefits of having breakfast every morning: It's said to reduce the risk of snacking on unhealthy foods throughout the day, decrease the risk of obesity and increase a child's ability to concentrate at school. The Dutch are champions of breakfast time and seem to be happier and healthier because of it. But the real point is that they put as much value on the idea of starting the day together around the breakfast table, a calming and bonding experience for all the family.

A healthy, balanced diet?

I was surprised that chocolate sprinkles are the centerpiece of breakfast across the Netherlands. Didn't the Dutch know about the importance of a well-balanced diet low in fat and sugar? It's true the Dutch have built a reputation, especially among expats, of preparing and eating stodgy, uninspiring food. Perhaps the best way to describe the Dutch approach to eating is that it's utilitarian: Foods should be easy and quick to prepare, affordable and nutritious. The only difference between a typical Dutch lunch and a typical Dutch breakfast is the three hours in between: Both are based on open sandwiches. Dinner, the only meal that is eaten hot, is often referred to as the holy trinity of meat, a vegetable and a car-bohydrate. Haute cuisine it ain't.

Yet, according to recent research, the Dutch no-nonsense approach to eating may be the way to go. An Oxfam study undertaken in 2014 declared that the Netherlands had "the best food in the world." Oxfam, an organization working to fight global poverty, looked at four cri-teria: whether there was a plentiful supply of food, how affordable it was, whether it was good quality, and whether it caused high rates of obesity and diabetes. The UK came in tenth. The US was way below, in twenty-first place, because although food in the US scored high in affordability and quality, the country's ranking was brought down by the high incidence of obesity and diabetes.

The UNICEF report supports Oxfam's claim. Dutch children had the lowest obesity rates of all the twenty-nine industrialized countries sur-veyed. Only 8.36 percent of Dutch children aged eleven, thirteen and fif-teen were deemed obese. Sadly, in every country except for three – the Netherlands, Denmark and Switzerland – childhood levels of obesity are now over 10 percent. The results show that the best place to eat in the world is not France, somewhere in the Mediterranean, or Japan, but right here in the Netherlands. In spite of all that butter, bread and *hagelslag*, the Dutch eat a healthy, balanced diet that's pretty much affordable to everyone.

This morning, as we watch our toddler happily eat his Dutch break-fast, his head swaying blissfully from side to side, his legs kicking to and fro, I finally realize what *hagelslag* is all about. Pausing for a moment and just looking at him, silencing all the neurotic and anxious voices in my head, I understand that, apart from his obvious enjoyment of the sweet taste of chocolate, my three-year-old son is content and proud to be able to choose and prepare his own breakfast. This translates into self-confidence. It really is all about the *hagelslag*.

Table manners maketh the child
Surely a culture that emphasizes the importance of the family eating

The tallest people in the world

The average height in Holland for a woman is five foot eight; for a man, it's six foot one. The low ceilings in old Dutch houses tell us that the population wasn't always so tall but, halfway through the nineteenth century, the Dutch started growing, and ceiling heights grew higher, too. There are lots of theories as to why the Dutch are so tall. Here are some of them:

- So they can keep their heads above water (26 percent of the country is below sea level and 29 percent is susceptible to river flooding)

- It must be all the cheese, milk and meat they consume (growth hormones and so on).

- Lack of stress (stress in childhood has been shown to affect growth)

- Reproduction of the "fittest": Women prefer to mate with taller men.

- People who live on the plains (i.e., a flat country) are taller; examples are the Masai, the Tuareg and the Fulani. Flatlanders are naturally tall, just as mountain folk are naturally small.

- Prosperity: When the GNP rises, so does the average height of the population.

- More "quiet sleep" (see Chapter 3)

- *Hagelslag* for breakfast!

together would have some cultural norms and practices that define behavior at the dinner table. The act of sitting down together and breaking bread regularly as a family is an important part of Dutch family life. At the very least, most Dutch families eat two daily meals together – breakfast and dinner. The young, as well as the old, are expected to follow a few common rules of courtesy to help create a *gezellig* environment – that Dutch feeling of coziness – conducive to the art of conversation. But is there anything particularly Dutch about them?

Naturally, I go to my resident expert in all matters pertaining to Dutch culture – my husband. "I can think of only one phrase that all children in the Netherlands grow up hearing: *'handen boven tafel'* (hands above the table)," responds Bram. "When sitting at the table, your hands are supposed to be above the table at all times, with your knife in your right hand and your fork in your left. Elbows on the table are definitely frowned upon."

Everyone – children included – is expected to wait until each person is at the table to begin eating. Waiting to eat until everyone has gathered is not only a sign of respect, but also creates a sense of community – every person counts, young as well as old. This is reinforced by the formality of everyone wishing each other *"Smakelijk eten"* (Enjoy your food/Bon appétit) before anyone lifts their fork. When leaving the table, it is considered polite to excuse oneself. It goes without saying that, as soon as they are old enough to sit at the table, kids are expected to keep their mouths closed while eating, and not to make any lip-smacking sounds.

In which Michele argues that it's actually all about the table

I'd held quite a few dinner parties when I was living in London, so I was used to cooking for large numbers before I moved to the Netherlands. The first piece of furniture I ever bought was a large dining table. I had quite a few friends who worked here, so when I first moved over, I was expecting to carry on having people over for dinner. I'd lived in various parts of France over the years and, always, the locals had welcomed me into their homes and we had all sat down together to eat. I had no reason to expect that Amsterdam would be any different.

I arrived and had my baby. I waited and waited, but no invitations came. Even people I had invited to eat with us didn't invite us back. After a while, I decided that, although Dutch people were incredibly friendly while doing business, they didn't necessarily want to socialize outside work hours. What's more, social networking at dinner parties, which is part of what drives at least the professional classes in London, was a foreign concept to them. What I hadn't understood was that the Dutch have a completely different attitude to the evening meal. A little too late to prevent me feeling just slightly upset, *The UnDutchables* finally shed some light on the matter: "Dinner is time for the family, which is why you are not invited. It's more usual to be invited for early drinks or a coffee."[1] I had, in fact, often been invited to early drinks – the *borrel* at 5:00 PM – but I found it strange that you were expected to leave before dinner.

In the Netherlands, the dinner table is a private, not a social, place. Funnily enough, in my work as a translator, *table* is a word that I notice keeps popping up in Dutch expressions. It seems deeply rooted in the culture. It recurs frequently in expressions such as *aan tafel gaan zitten met iemand* (to sort something out between you), *ter tafel komen* (to raise for discussion) or *iets boven tafel krijgen* (to get something out into the open). The table is where everything is sorted out, where disagreements are settled, views shared and new agreements made. Roundtable discussions are a common format for television talk shows: There's nothing more Dutch than a selection of semicelebrities and experts sitting around a table enjoying a lively debate. *Gezellig*.

The dinner table is the place where children learn to have their own opinions and express them. Conversation is an intrinsic part of the family dynamic. "We believe it's crucial to take the time to have breakfast and dinner together, so we can listen to each other, share our experiences, talk about what's going on in the world and put it into a wider context," Carel van Eck, a Dutch father of two, tells me. "Breakfast conversation typically turns out to be news-related: We browse the paper during breakfast, comment on key events and chat about what the kids have coming up at school and after school. During dinner, conversation is more geared toward events of the day. What happened? How did you react? What did you learn?"

Back home in the UK, breakfast may be a free-for-all, or skipped altogether, and it's common for children to have their "tea" and eat their fish fingers and chips in the late afternoon, while the parents have their own sit-down supper much later, at a civilized, continental time, often once the children are in bed. Here in the Netherlands, the whole family sits down to eat together at six o'clock. Given the timing, fancy cuisine is out of the question, so it's usually something simple or food that's been prepared over the weekend and can be reheated. The practice of eating together as a family means that working parents leave the office on time as a matter of unquestioned right.

Dit zijn we (This is who we are), a book on Dutch traditions, mentions the typical food you'll find on a Dutch table. Simplicity is key. For lunch, an open sandwich with some kind of savory topping – often ham or cheese – is usually followed by *boterham tevredenheid* (sandwich of satisfaction!), plain bread and butter, which you fill up on. The Dutch often drink buttermilk (yuck) with their lunch and sometimes with dinner, too. While the diet may not look healthy at first glance, the Dutch are not prone to excess. Their natural frugality has influenced social mores: Only one biscuit may be taken from the tin if you are invited for coffee; if you are invited for the *borrel*, the host will spread little crackers with cheese or paté and hand them out. This rationing ensures that control is maintained over how much everyone eats.

One day a week is often dedicated to finishing up leftovers. Stale bread is recycled into delicious *wentelteefjes*, a kind of French toast. For dinner, *stamppot* (potatoes mashed with cabbage or kale) is a common staple, along with sausages and gravy. We often eat this at home.

The Dutch are also keen on soups, stews and casseroles. They're quick to prepare, easy to reheat and nourishing. Sometimes my husband will cook multiple dishes on a Sunday to prepare us for the week.

How to make *wentelteefjes*

Ingredients: 1 egg, 1 cup of vanilla-flavored sugar (or sugar and vanilla extract), ground cinnamon (to taste), 1 cup of milk, stale sliced bread, pat of butter*

Preparation: Beat together in a shallow bowl the egg, vanilla sugar, cinnamon and milk. Cut the crusts off the bread, and dip the slices one by one into the mixture. Stack them up and pour any leftover mixture on them. Melt the butter in a large pan. Pan fry the slices for about five minutes, turning halfway through. Serve and enjoy!

Some recipes also include adding a dash of rum or orange juice to the mixture.

In the Netherlands, sitting down around the table as a family is less about what's on the table than the fact of sitting around it to talk. A family dinner is about *gezelligheid*. Many Dutch parents see it as a basic rule: The family eats together. Anne, my Dutch friend who moved to London, noticed the cultural difference, too. "Something that struck me here is that families don't have dinner together often. Children have an early kids'-type meal (fish fingers, baked beans, etc.) by themselves, maybe with a parent present, but very often dished up in front of the TV. Traditionally, a Dutch family will all eat together and chat about their day as equals. Could it be a reason for Dutch children being more at ease with talking to grown-ups?"

Research undertaken in the US has shown that the way a family dines is a powerful predictor of how children will develop: Kids who eat dinner with their parents at least five times a week were less likely, as teenagers, to smoke, drink, use marijuana, get into serious fights, have sex, or be suspended from school. They also did better at school and were more likely to go on to college.[2]

In spite of the basic rules of table manners, there's little formality to a Dutch dinner table, which makes conversation easier. In the sixteenth century, Hadrianus Julius was commissioned to write the first known study of Dutch identity. His view was that "Hollanders are too blunt and rude for the higher forms of civilization." Herman Pleij also mentions the historical lack of courtly manners. After all, there was no Dutch court; instead, there was a decentralized government structure. As a consequence, the Dutch do not stand on ceremony, and they believe most formal etiquette to be nonsense. Pleij explains: "We find [etiquette] totally unnecessary. We prefer to get down to business as quickly as possible without wasting time on meaningless formalities." So, while there are basic table manners to be obeyed, as Rina explained earlier, none of these things should get in the way of a good conversation.

As Professor Ruut Veenhoven said to us when we talked to him, what could be more different from dinner in the Netherlands than the tableau of a French family dining together? Let's pause to imagine this for a second. It's late in the evening, there is intricate and sometimes challenging food on the table, and the French children are expected to sit there and neatly put away an adult meal. Slip across the border to the Netherlands, and you have an early dinner, simple food and children chatting away with their parents about their day. What child wouldn't prefer this? The Dutch approach contributes to good, open communication within the family as well as clear rules, structure and produces, and as a consequence, happy children.

12

Let's Talk about Sex

In which Michele is asked some embarrassing questions

I've been following with interest the newspaper columns written by Pia de Jong, a Dutch writer currently based in Princeton, New Jersey, with her family. It's always fascinating to follow the culture clash the other way around: How do Dutch people find life abroad? It turns out that, unsurprisingly, the US is the polar opposite of the Netherlands in some respects. Recently, Pia wrote that the school had her sign a form promising to discuss sexual abstinence with her teenage daughter. She went on to explain that some states insist that all information about contraception should include emphasis on the negative and unhealthy consequences of sex. The premise is that sex can make you ill, so the only safe option is not to have it.

In the Netherlands, on the other hand, it seems that teen sex is very much tolerated, and most teenagers have their first sexual experience in the safety of the parental home. Research indicates that, on average, teens in the Netherlands do *not* have sex at an earlier age than those in other European countries or in the US, even though society and parents are more permissive.[1] When they did have sex for the first time, a Rutgers University study found, nine out of ten Dutch adolescents used contraceptives. According to the 2013 UNICEF report, 75 percent of Dutch teenagers use a condom the first time they have sex, and data from the World Health Organization shows that Dutch teens are among the top users of the birth control pill. As a result, there are fewer teenage pregnancies.

The picture couldn't be any more different in our own countries, with the US topping the charts of all the developed nations for the most teenage pregnancies between the ages of fifteen and nineteen. New Zealand, England and Wales complete the top four.[2] I wondered how many British and American kids lose their virginity at home.

Of course, sex can be a tricky, embarrassing topic. "No sex, please, we're British" was the climate I grew up in. It was all nudge nudge, wink wink and silly innuendo. You couldn't really talk about it openly, and certainly not with your parents. Sex education was something you were taught at school in an embarrassing biology lesson. It was being given a coy book containing pictures of the birds and bees, the old-fashioned version of today's *Where Willy Went*. I'm pretty sure I never discussed anything to do with sex with my mother. Most of my information came from an older girl. We hid in a changing-room cubicle one swimming lesson and she told me all the gory facts of life. When I was a teenager, my father once left a pile of leaflets about contraception next to my bed, but no mention was ever made of them. Here, though, I've been inspired by the way Dutch parents educate their children about sex. There's no one significant show-and-tell moment, just a continuing response to the child's progressive curiosity about the body, with a focus on sensuality as well as sexuality, and clear information about respect and boundaries.

While schools provide age-appropriate lessons on intimacy and sexuality, the rule for parents is that nothing should be kept from children and that there are no taboo subjects. The idea is to answer any questions, simply and honestly, as they arise, at the child's level of understanding and maturity. It was one of the first pieces of parenting advice I received from other parents here: So many people mentioned this pragmatic approach to me that I can't place exactly when or where I first heard it.

Spring fever week

Lentekriebels week is more literally (and amusingly) translated as "spring itches week." Each spring, Dutch primary schools take part in a week-long national sex-education program aimed at children between the ages of four and twelve. The youngest have lessons on topics like falling in love. Older children are taught about the changes to their bodies and social and emotional development, as well as about safe sex and consent.[3]

The aim of these lessons is:

- To give children a positive self-image and develop their skills in the area of relationships and sexuality

- To ensure that young people are well equipped with knowledge about sex before they enter puberty, so they take fewer risks

- To teach them to think about friendship, love and relationships, not just physical changes and reproduction. It also gives them a safe code of conduct

I recently asked my sister-in-law Sabine how she handled the topic with her children. A fashion designer living in the coastal town of Heemstede, her youngest child is now seventeen. She said, "We always talked about sex openly but, to be honest, I never really sat down with them to explain everything. Most of it came about through answering their random questions as and when they arose."

The puberty guide handed out to parents of all ten-year-olds by the health service states that children who have a good relationship with their parents tend to wait longer before having sex. Interestingly enough, the term "underage sex" doesn't appear in the book at all. The legal age of consent in the Netherlands is sixteen, but exceptions are made for consensual acts between adolescents close in age. In the UK the age of consent is sixteen, while in the US it ranges from sixteen to eighteen, depending on the state.

When I first moved to Amsterdam, I was shocked when I heard that Dutch parents allow their teenage children to have friends of the opposite sex stay the night. Yet this chimes with the Dutch cultural tendency to show a tolerant attitude. It's the same accepting but controlling tolerance they have toward soft drugs and prostitution, for example. Teenage sex is allowed, but they prefer it to be in a controlled environment, that is, under the teen's parents' own roof. It is highly likely that a safe place to have sex encourages safe sex.

Let's be clear: The attitude is not "anything goes." There are still rules to follow, agreed upon between the parents and their children.

Sabine tells me that she told each of her children that she wasn't ready to become a grandmother yet, so they should be sensible: "I've always said that someone could stay the night if she or he had been over during the day first, so that I could get to know them. It's not the intention that they bring someone new home at the end of a night out. Maybe I'm a bit old-fashioned, but I'd hate to be suddenly confronted with a teenager I'd never met before at the breakfast table."

In practice, things have been fairly straightforward with her children. Her two sons, the eldest of whom is nineteen, haven't brought that many girlfriends home, and her twenty-one-year-old daughter has been in a long-term relationship for several years: "They've been together for ages, but at the beginning her boyfriend didn't stay over. One night he did try to drunkenly shin up her drainpipe at three in the morning with a friend and they made it on to her balcony. Incredibly dangerous. But typical Joosje, she herself sent them packing again . . . through the front door."

I talked to another Dutch friend, who asked to remain anonymous in order not to embarrass her daughter. She tells me her daughter went on the pill when she was fifteen. It was ostensibly to help reduce her pimples, though my friend qualifies this with, "But they really weren't that bad." Not long afterward, her daughter started going out with her first boyfriend, who was the same age as her. "That made it easier. It was like they were discovering things together. I'd have had a problem with it if he had been much older than her." The fact that her daughter was below the official Dutch age of consent didn't arise, as her boyfriend was the same age. After about two months, she told me, he started staying the night. My friend didn't mind – she reckoned they would have had sex anyway, and it was safer under their own roof – but it took her husband a longer time to come around, having grown up in the more conservative, southern part of the country. I asked how she had told her daughter about sex. "There wasn't a particular tell-all moment. They get so much from books and films. I think that particular culture has blown over from Scandinavia." I agree: Dutch children's books go into sex and intimacy in a lot more detail than British or American ones. My eight-year-old daughter has just read a book aimed at seven- to nine-year-olds, which includes a scene in which the main character, a little boy, comes across his divorcée mother and her new girlfriend having sex in the living room.[4]

Historical openness about sex

A book on Dutch traditions written by Ineke Strouken gives me a better understanding of how the Dutch developed such a healthy and accepting attitude toward sex.[5] The Dutch have long been open about it, and have allowed men and women the freedom to choose their partners. Speed dating isn't a modern invention here – it's been the trend since 1573. The Dutch had informal fairs called *Meidenmarkten* (maidens' markets) and *Vrijersmarkten* (suitors' markets), during which young people could meet suitable partners. Contact would be fairly direct, with kissing and fondling in the dunes allowed on the day they met, with, hopefully, a marriage proposal following. Until the middle of the last century, it was normal for communities to have a dedicated lovers' meeting place, for example, the lane behind the church. There might also be a *billenavond* (literally, a "buttock evening"), when any girl wearing violets could be kissed without her permission being asked first.

Nachtvrijen (nighttime courting) was a custom common in the seventeenth and eighteenth centuries among the lower classes. Back then, it seems it was quite normal for boys to climb in through a girl's window and have sex with her. (Presumably, my niece's boyfriend had heard about this. Or he'd been reading Shakespeare.) This lusty behavior is also evident in the work of domestic genre painters of the Golden Age, especially that of Jan Steen. And at the end of the Second World War, the sexually forward behavior of Dutch women on Liberation Day was so shocking to some Yankee soldiers that special guidelines had to be issued. So there is some historical background to the liberal reputation the Dutch enjoy today.

Difficult questions

My children are the curious type. My son, Ben, in particular, wants to know *everything*. I have been answering their questions on anatomy and reproduction from almost as early as they could talk. This has led to some pretty embarrassing moments. Ben was delighted when his little sister, Ina, was born, and eagerly helped change her diaper. Consequently, my two-and-a-half-year-old became interested in female genitalia. So I explained what the different parts were and told him their appropriate anatomical names. He then wanted to know what the various parts were for. Later, in polite company, he suddenly asked, "Mummy, so does it hurt your clitoris when I sit on your lap?" There was more laughter than embarrassment (aside from my own).

Living in Amsterdam, we have inevitably on several occasions walked and cycled past prostitutes in their red-lit windows. The children showed increasing interest as they grew older, but then it waned. Together, we have read articles in the paper about prostitutes paying tax, about human trafficking and modern-day slavery. Discussions have ensued about the rights and wrongs of prostitution. The same goes for child marriages: My daughter even has views on this, believing currently that it might be better to escape a war-torn country through marriage, even with all that entails long-term. My children are well-informed and take a broad-minded view on sexual matters, yet they are also aware that some things are wrong. They know what pedophilia is but, as Ben says, these are people with an illness who need help, not to be ostracized.

At primary school, my children have had lessons on physical intimacy and personal boundaries, which reinforced the idea that it's OK to say no if you are uncomfortable with anything, be it in a sexual context, or just in play. In fact, the hardest things to explain to my children haven't been sex-related but cultural: Because they've grown up in a mostly secular society, it's taken more effort to explain religious beliefs to them. And in this egalitarian society, class has been another concept that has drawn a blank. "What does 'posh' mean, Mummy?"

I have found myself surfing naked pictures of men and women with Ben after a conversation about sperm donors had led to a discussion of pornographic magazines and the natural question of what they looked like. Sometimes, I worry I have taken Dutch parenting too far in my rigorous application of the liberal, unembarrassed approach. Recent questions from my son, who is just a couple of years shy of becoming a fully fledged teen, include: "Is sex fun? How? What do gay men actually do? How does a sperm donor get the sperm out? What kind of magazine do they get if they don't know if they fancy men or women? How did you masturbate as a child?" Eek. And this is why, sometimes, you long for someone else to explain all these things to your kids, rather than having to do it yourself. That's where Dr. Corrie comes in: She is a Dutch TV institution.

The Dr. Corrie Show, shown on Sundays at 6:15 PM, is aimed at children from nine to twelve years old. Half comedy, half documentary, the (madly irritating) buck-toothed Dr. Corrie talks to teenagers and celebrity guests about sex and explains things with the help of plastic models, cartoon diagrams and volunteers. Subjects covered include sexiness, homosexuality, condoms, puberty, sex and the internet, being in love, setting boundaries, nakedness, masturbation and kissing. There's a no-holds-barred, no-nonsense approach that aims to leave children entertained, well informed and able to act responsibly. Ben and his friends have seen almost all the episodes, but Ina would much rather watch something else, like football. In my opinion, she simply isn't ready for this information yet.

Sex exhibits at the museum

This week, Ben's school had a teacher-training day, so one of his new friends suggested that five of them go to the science museum together. Perched on top of the tunnel that takes traffic from the center of Amsterdam to the northern suburbs, NEMO is a children's science museum filled with interactive science and technology exhibits. It's not something I would have done unaccompanied at his age but, then again, I led a sheltered childhood out in the sticks. There weren't any exciting museums where I lived. These city kids are brave enough to venture out without parents and are all pleasantly nerdy enough to want to visit a museum.

I'd been to the museum before. It's *very* interactive. You can step inside a massive soap bubble, use hydraulics to work your own elevator or put together an extensive electronic circuit. I also know that there is a hands-on educational exhibit called "Teen Facts" that allows you to get a feel for French kissing, for example, by putting your hand into a sock puppet inside a box and having someone else do the same from the opposite side. I asked Ben whether they planned to go up to that floor, which also has a section designed to resemble a sex shop, and he said, "Sure."

When they got back, I probed a little, and asked Ben what he'd thought of the section on puberty. "I knew most of that stuff already, Mum. I mean, I know what a vulva is." When I inquired about the section dealing specifically with sex, he looked a little apologetic. "We didn't really like that. There were condoms, which I hadn't seen before – only in pictures – but also dildos. Eeeuw!" He admits almost sheepishly that they'd whipped through the section on sex toys pretty quick. "None of us was that interested. I think it was meant for older children."

So what is it that everyone is so worried about? When healthy interests are cultivated, children are generally capable of dealing with age-appropriate information. If there is no secrecy, shame or embarrassment around the topic, children will decide for themselves how much they want to know. Research suggests that cultivating sexual taboos leads to sexual fixations and a "forbidden fruit" complex. It's also been suggested that furtive, hurried childhood masturbation can lead to physical conditioning – for example, programming men when grown up to have problems with premature ejaculation. No one wishes that for their son.

I also believe it's better to avoid teaching children to be embarrassed about their naked bodies. Small children play naked on my street in the height of the summer. Ina and her friend Tijn were still stripping off for the wading pool in the allotment last summer at the age of eight. A boy and a girl playing innocently with water. Happy kids.

Gender issues

It wouldn't really be fair to say that my children are typical in their tastes and hobbies, even in the Netherlands. For example, at three years old, Ben came home from the crèche one day and asked whether he could start ballet classes. A little boy he'd been playing with had told him about it. Eight years later, Ben and that same friend, Angus, are preparing for their grade 4 Cecchetti exams at the same ballet school. Other boys have come and gone in the class. One of them, Ernst, became Ernesta and moved to the girls' ballet class. What would their journey have been back in *Billy Elliot* country? My stepsister has three daughters, all of whom compete in dance shows, and tells me that boys are warmly welcomed. They tend to give up at around the age of nine, though, affected, she feels, by the predominant football culture in the UK. "I think their dads have a lot to do with it. They want their sons to do football, since it's perceived as a bit odd if they don't."

There are theories that siblings develop their tastes and hobbies in contrast to each other. Perhaps this is the reason my daughter joined a football team four years ago. She is currently the only girl on a team of sporty boys. While Ben is in touch with his feminine side, Ina, the tomboy, has always gravitated toward playing with boys. Though she also likes dancing, she refused to join the girls' ballet class and was allowed into the boys' class (gender discrimination avoided) until the standard got too high for her, because the other boys were older.

One big sex-related issue I hear about in the English-speaking world these days is gendered marketing. The gendering debate has been raging on both sides of the Atlantic, with justified criticism of the way boys' and girls' toys and clothes have become polarized into pink and blue over the past few decades. Superheroes for boys; princesses for girls. In the UK, Mumsnet is filled with angry discussions about the impact of princessifying female childhood and its links to the early sexualization of girls. In 2010, the website launched its own campaign, "Let Girls Be Girls." The campaign aims "to curb the premature sexualization of children by asking retailers to commit not to sell products which play upon, emphasize or exploit their sexuality." Target announced in 2015 that it will stop labeling its toys as being for boys or for girls; their decision was met with enthusiasm and applause from one side, and complaints and resistance from the other.[6]

In an article in the *Telegraph* in 2007, journalist Sarah Womack described a "generation of damaged girls." She even drew a link between gendered marketing and UNICEF's first child well-being report, in 2007, in which British children ranked at the very bottom, as the "unhappiest and unhealthiest in the developed world."[7] The American Psychological Association donned its gloves, saying that "inappropriate marketing is leading to a sexualization of children by a consumer society."[8] But it's not as if the gendering of toys doesn't exist in the Netherlands. At dress-up day in a class of five-year-olds here, you'll also come across plenty of princesses and pirates, and toy shops have their pink and blue sections, too. Yet older Dutch children don't seem so polarized in their tastes or dress sense; neither do they seem overtly sexual at a young age.

I put the difference down to the absence of a prevalent lad culture. Dutch women are too confident and self-assured to let themselves be turned into male fantasies. Misogyny and the objectification of women is not found to the same extent in the polders of Holland. Every time I return to the UK now, I'm struck by how much makeup British women wear. I have to conclude that, despite the pink and blue toys, Dutch kids have healthier gender role models. The Netherlands is a country filled with strong, practical women and men who embrace housework, laundry and childcare as part and parcel of their job as fathers. Gay Pride is a long-standing major public event here, and homosexuality is rarely frowned upon. Same-sex marriages have been legal since 2001, and families that consist of two dads or two moms are officially recognized. As a result, children are exposed to the whole gamut of gender models from an early age.

When we met with political scientist and feminist Roos Wouters in the Amsterdam library, I discovered that her children defy gender models, too. "I've got a girlish boy and a boyish girl," she said. "My son really liked pink as a little boy. He wanted pink pajamas so I got him them. No problem with that. My daughter has always preferred toys like building blocks and cars and she had a real issue with princess-y stuff. Now she's eleven and still wears boy's clothes, but she has grown her hair. The other kids have stopped placing girls and boys in separate boxes, so I think she feels less of a need to kick against it."

We ended up discussing what might be counteracting the negative influence of gendered toys and clothing. At secondary school here, you often see boys wearing jewelry, and pink or floral patterns, while a lot of girls wear jeans and little makeup. There seems to be just one conclusion to draw: It's down to the good example of their adult role models – those practically minded, practically dressed Dutch parents.

13

Dutch Teenagers Don't Rebel

In which Michele thinks about the future

Ben has reached the age where people are always commenting on how grown up he is. His cheekbones and chin have become more angular, his shoulders have broadened and, though he hasn't shot up yet, puberty is well on its way. He is also self-sufficient and independent. He has to be. Although there is plenty of after-school care available for primary school children, in the form of subsidized after-school clubs, at secondary school a Dutch twelve-year-old is expected to be able to make his own way to and from school on his bike, and do his homework on his own before his parents arrive back from work.[1]

Looking ahead at the years to come, I'm keen to continue my consciously relaxed parenting approach. But I wonder whether adolescent hormones might end the current peace and tranquillity. Ben is already starting to act up on occasion, and the onset of puberty is clearly affecting his moods. Sundays, in particular, can be difficult, when he doesn't have a fixed routine and tends to be tired and grumpy. Like most parents, I'm worried about what adolescence will bring. I'm also concerned about keeping the dialogue open. I want my son to continue to confide in me, the way he has always done.

My own experience of Dutch teenagers has been nothing but positive. My sister-in-law's three children – two boys and a girl – are a decade older than mine. I've never seen them being anything other than pleasant, polite and comfortable in adult company. They seem open and friendly at all times, never sulky, belligerent or moody. The various teenage babysitters we've had have all been lovely. Our fifteen-year-old newspaper delivery boy is always smiling and polite.

What do I have to do in order that Ben turns into one of those pleasant, polite Dutch teenagers I see around the place? They seem confident enough to go about dressed in cool but unsexy clothing. And they don't seem to feel the need to battle with their elders. Will the culture alone work its magic? The teenagers here certainly look very different to the oversexualized, skimpily dressed kids I see in Britain. Though there are plenty of arguments in favor of school uniforms, I've noticed that British children who wear them feel compelled to assert their identity outside school in extreme ways. At least, that's how I reacted myself when I was a schoolgirl – it was all black, ripped clothing, chains and heavy makeup. (The fourteen-year-old me was slightly ridiculous.) Here, there are no school uniforms, but the kids all wear the same uniform anyway: jeans and sneakers. And Ben assures me he hasn't ever come across anyone being bullied at school for what they had on.

When I handed my mother the photograph of Ben's new class, she did a double take because she'd half expected they'd be wearing a uniform. After that, she tried to count how many boys and girls there were in his class, but struggled to see the difference, because a lot of them had the same gender-neutral haircuts and clothing. It seems that if you give children a bike and let them choose their own clothes, they will make practical choices. Perhaps, not having a school uniform, these kids don't need to assert their individuality or prove a point? Perhaps in a society where sexuality is accepted as natural and teenagers are well informed, they don't need to express their sexuality in inappropriate, provocative ways? Perhaps fewer rules mean less rebellion? From the outside, it appears that Dutch teenagers don't rebel.

As a whole, the Dutch are not rebellious. They have a historical reputation for sobriety. Are sober people happier? If you are a conformist, does that make you more content? Or is it that if you are a happy person, you don't feel the need to challenge the norms? Does being Dutch mean always staying on an even keel and never giving in to passionate behavior? Like the Germans and the Scandinavians, the Dutch are seen as the opposite of those fiery southern Europeans. But then I remember the Dutch beer-drinking culture, the wild goings-on at *Carnaval* (Mardi Gras) in the south, and the unrestrained passion at football matches. The Dutch certainly aren't sober and sensible all of the time.

Simon Kuper wrote a perceptive article for the *Financial Times* comparing the parenting of teenagers in the Netherlands with that in the US. He explains how Dutch parents create "zones of order" in which teenage experimentation is tolerated but monitored and controlled by the parents – for example, allowing them to have sex at home: "Dutch parents treat teen sex much as Dutch society treats drugs or prostitution: Permit it, hug it close, control it." Americans, on the other hand, try to enforce good behavior by punishing transgressions. All this means is that they have created a vicious cycle where socially unacceptable behavior like taking illegal drugs and having promiscuous sex is driven underground and so becomes more enticing to teenagers, precisely because it is forbidden. "The Netherlands has done everything humanly possible to make teen sex and drugs seem dull," Kuper writes. "American social conservatives should try it out."[2]

Recently, I happened to be discussing Dutch teenagers with a couple of fellow expat translators at one of our frequent get-togethers. One mentioned how astonished she'd been to see a teenage girl walking along the street hand in hand with her mother. The other commented on how different this was from the UK, where, in her eyes, children are overprotected until they're about twelve and then allowed completely free rein. "At which point, they try to spend as little time with their parents as possible," she added. When I think back to my own teenage years, I can remember being let loose by my mother, but with a whole stack of rules in my back pockets – rules that were nonnegotiable. Parents were generally seen as the enemy. "It's not like here, where teenagers do things with their parents and happily go on holiday with them." This struck a chord with me: When I was a teenager, family vacations were my idea of a nightmare, and I stopped going along when I was fifteen.

Leafing through the papers last weekend, I was stopped in my tracks by a large BMW advertisement featuring a blond Dutch family of five, the eldest child clearly much taller than his father. Photos showed the family eating out together, playing boccie, driving along in the car. Although this is a projection of an ideal, it's still ideal in which teenagers participate fully in family life. That said, it's not *all* roses. Dutch parents do complain about their teenage kids, in predictable fashion. Columnist Sylvia Witteman tweeted:

7:02 PM, 11 July 2014: I've got a bevy of adolescents in the house who've been honing the concept of "apathy" for days.[3]

Anglo-Dutch documentary filmmaker Sunny Bergman blogs about her struggles with her adolescent children. She brought them up on sugar-free diets, Astrid Lindgren books and deep philosophical conversation, only to find them now addicted to silly YouTube vlogs and cheesy music:

> A message to all parents of small children: You can try your hardest but it can still all be in vain . . . all of a sudden those fairy-tale infants turn into adolescents, lying on the sofa, glued to their screens. They needed mobile phones to be able to WhatsApp their classmates about homework but, if they can, all they'll do is watch vlogs nonstop.[4]

Bergman goes on to explain what these vloggers like to do – for example, lie in a bath of a sponsored soft drink, demonstrate how to give yourself a deodorant burn on your wrists, or how to make yourself puke by eating bananas followed by Sprite. It sounds like typical teenage behavior to me. It's rather a relief to discover that, inside the privacy of their own homes, those polite Dutch kids are actually quite normal. Still, their behavior in public needs some explanation. In any case, how do Dutch parents manage to have such a great relationship with their teenage kids? Is it because of their high tolerance? I decide to seek some parenting advice on the subject.

The first advice I'm given is unsolicited. Between the ages of ten and eleven, all Dutch children are called up for a health and growth check at their local health clinic. Ben is almost eleven by the time he is summoned. We wait for hours until it's our turn. The nurse is an older woman dressed in the colorful fashion I associate with hippie shops that sell India-inspired clothes and incense. It soon becomes clear why she is running behind schedule; she's a chatterbox, spending a long time asking Ben about his hobbies. Neither Ben nor I can tell whether this long preamble is small talk or whether she's doing some kind of psychological assessment. We look at each other, puzzled.

Ben is measured and weighed. At school, there is much excitement about this check-up, because at it the children are given a height prediction. Ben comes out at the average for the Netherlands, predicted to reach six foot one (184 cm) as an adult. Not bad for a boy who is only 12.5 percent genetically Dutch (one half-Dutch, half-German grandparent, one Hungarian grandparent, and two English ones). Maybe there is something in the milk, after all. When this part is over, the nurse asks him in a rather theatrical manner, "And do you know what's going to happen next?" Ben looks scared. What was she getting at? What was she going to do to him? More vaccinations?

She spins her chair round to face a cupboard behind her, takes out a red book and hands it to him. PUBERTY is written in large letters across the front.

"That's right! You're going to go through puberty!" she says, as if she's announcing a surprise party.

Ben looks bemused and hands me the book, plus a leaflet containing illustrations of genital growth. He's happier with the postcard that says, "Target height: 184cm." Later, when I turn the card over, I see that PUBERTY is also written on the front of the card. Just to make sure you don't forget to go through it.

The puberty guide begins:

Dear Parents,

Your child has reached puberty. During puberty, children grow into a new identity. They develop into adult human beings. They don't just grow physically but also emotionally and in their way of thinking . . . Some parents find puberty a difficult phase. But your interest in your child's world and your support remain important.

It's full of useful information I really *didn't* know. For example, that kids' eyeballs grow during growth spurts, which can cause eye pain and headaches, or that teenage boys, as well as girls, now shave off their pubic hair. (I can't wait for Ben to get his first Brazilian.) There's advice on when to call your child in sick: only when they are running a temperature (above 100 degrees Fahrenheit) and not when they simply have a stomachache or a headache. A child with these symptoms is usually better off at school, the health authority claims.

The guide advises parents not to comment on adolescents should they choose to wear wacky clothes. If you do, it will make them want to emphasize their autonomy by dressing even more extremely. (Hello, fourteen-year-old Michele.) The advice to avoid direct confrontation reminds me that my friends Heleen and Thomas told me the word "no" is avoided in the Netherlands. The guide also mentions how important it is that parents set a good example. Adolescents are quick to notice if you say one thing and do another. "Of course, parents are only human and sometimes make mistakes. But, in general, they should set a good example for their children. Otherwise, all those little parenting chats will be pointless. More important: The child will carry the norms you set in the back of his mind for the rest of his life."[5]

There is advice on encouraging hygiene. I think Ben's already got to the point of needing to be encouraged. If I left him to his own devices, I don't think he would ever take a bath or a shower. And on emotional development: "Young people can develop in an emotionally stable way if their parents have clear and realistic expectations of them and respect their independence."[6] Fair enough.

Parents are encouraged to have trust in their child:

He often doesn't need your permission anymore. Most adolescents *don't* hang out with the wrong crowd, don't use drugs and aren't mouthy. On the contrary, the majority of adolescents are happy to spend time at home and love their parents. Research has shown this. The generation gap isn't as great as you might think.

Dutch children generally do have an excellent relationship with their parents. In the Children's Life Satisfaction section of the 2013 UNICEF report, the researchers concluded that good family relationships were the single most important contributor to subjective well-being, whereas, for example, in France, one in four teenagers reported having difficulty talking to their parents.

While some earlier generations in the Low Countries did clash with their stricter parents – for example, in the Youth Rebellion of the 1960s – there is very little intergenerational conflict these days. Society is less authoritarian and family life is more democratic. There simply isn't as much to rebel against.

Trust

I decide to compare the theory with what is happening in practice. My initial port of call, as ever, is my sister-in-law Sabine. The first thing she has to say about parenting teenagers is this: "The one thing I continue to believe in is to keep talking to them, to keep on repeating the consequences of certain behaviors, of the use of drugs and alcohol or social media. And to trust them and, more importantly, have them realize how important it is for me to be able to keep on trusting them."

Research has linked trust to happiness. It's an important factor. Sabine tells me you have to build trust between you and your children: As they grow up and become more independent, you have to trust them to cycle to school on their own and return home safely. You have to trust them not to do anything foolish or dangerous, and to take responsibility for their own safety and actions. The degree of trust grows with your child: The older they become, the more you have to let them go.

I ask Sabine about the rules she has for her teenagers. The one most important to her turns out to be no screen time before 5:00 PM. She feels it encourages the kids to play outside or do their homework: "And, let's be honest, getting a bit bored isn't that bad for them either!" Apart from that, there aren't strict rules about what time her teenagers have to come home – it depends on what their plans are – but on the whole she expects them to be home by six for dinner.

The general feeling among Dutch parents is that rules should be worked out with the child, with both parties agreeing they are reasonable. Dialogue is key. While, in the 1960s, the youth revolution led to an age of permissiveness and antiauthoritarian thinking, the pendulum has now swung back, and today's Dutch parents do set some boundaries – but in consultation with their children. In *Opvoeden in een verwenmaatschappij* (Parenting in a pampered society), Marijke Bisschop argues that too few rules make for spoiled kids, and many other parenting experts would agree with that.

In her view, children should be encouraged to become independent, self-reliant and responsible. Adolescents need to learn to solve problems on their own and take responsibility for their own actions. One important lesson is that other people aren't always the reason for your problems – the cause might lie in yourself, so if you want things to change you should start with yourself. She also says that many parents set the bar too high. Expectations shouldn't be unrealistic. Spoiling, or "helicoptering," being pushed to do things, being constantly supervised and overscheduled, could make children insecure, weak, moany, helpless, dependent, indecisive, complacent, frustrated, intolerant, discontented, unhappy, vulnerable and lacking in respect!

In terms of practical advice, Bisschop advises mothers not to look for things their teenagers have lost and not to replace them. I resolve to try this. If Ben loses his phone, I'm going to let him "feel the pain." If I constantly offer solutions to problems of his own making, he will never learn to take responsibility for his actions. An opportunity arises when he loses the key to his bike lock at school for the third time. I tell him I'm too busy working to come and pick him up and he'll have to make sure his bike isn't stolen. With practical impracticality, he decides to carry (or rather drag) his locked bike home, which leads to a ripped back tire and the bike spending the next two days at the repair shop. The key is found a week later. Three months' pocket money goes to a new tire.

Bisschop also suggests a way of developing your child's sense of responsibility: Let him organize his own outings. She also outlines some basic rules to minimize mess in your child's bedroom, which I decide to adapt for our family and implement at once.

Following the new rules makes Ben feel in control of his room. Unfortunately, I still have to nag him to turn off his light and open his curtains. No daylight would shine into his room if he had his own way; perhaps he has become part vampire. There are still piles of clothes on the floor most of the week but, surprisingly, he does at some point put them in the laundry basket. The puberty guide advises me *not* to dilute the effects of compliments for good behavior (room-tidying is given as an example) by adding, "I wish you'd do your best *all the time*." They've got us parents figured out.

House rules for teenagers

- No food leftovers, dirty plates, cans or bottles in the bedroom

- No clothes on the floor

- Put dirty clothes into the laundry basket at least once a week.

- Keep the door closed (so parents don't have to see the mess).

- Hang up wet towels to dry.

The development of the teenage brain

During an introductory parents' evening at Ben's new school, I meet his homeroom teacher, Lydwin. According to Ben, she's the coolest teacher ever: Not only does she have piercings, but she used to sing in a metal band and she teaches astronomy. I feel irredeemably old and boring by comparison. Lydwin, who is indeed young and cool-looking, and very pleasant, gives a talk to the parents about the transition from primary to secondary school. Our children are confronted with a new world and different expectations, she says. Homework is the main difference between primary and secondary school, and she asks the parents in the room how long their children are spending on it before telling us that the median answer – three quarters of an hour a day – would be a good rule of thumb. Any longer, and it's a sign that they need help to plan their homework assignments better across the week. (The school will provide this help.) She is emphatic that homework should not be done at the expense of sports, hobbies and recreational activities.

The pupils will take regular tests, which will be divided into two sections: one, knowledge; the other, the application of that knowledge. These are different skill sets. Up to the age of around thirteen, children's brains are still developing the ability to apply knowledge, so some may not have matured enough yet to do so. "It's important for the school to identify children who are struggling with this," she says, "so that they can offer specific help." I am pleasantly surprised by this approach, having heard of sink-or-swim scenarios at the older Dutch *gymnasia*. Having mentioned intellectual development, Lydwin then recommends we read the influential book *Het puberende brein* (*The Adolescent Brain*) by Eveline Crone, which is credited with changing the way teenagers are regarded here. It will help us understand their motivations, limitations and capabilities.

A week later, I cycle to the library and borrow the book. It's not so much a parenting guide as an explanation of the neurological development of the adolescent brain. Eveline Crone is professor in the department of developmental and educational psychology at Leiden University. The book is rather technical, and hasn't been translated into English, but here's my attempt to pick out the most relevant bits: Adolescence is a time when relationships with friends become all-important, leading to peer pressure and a desire to conform. At the same time, adolescent hormones are getting into gear, and the brain is full of hormone receptors, so emotions are intensified. Think of Romeo and Juliet.

Crone explains that typical adolescent behavior can be explained by the fact that development does not take place evenly across the brain. Social reasoning and rational thinking are two of the last areas to develop. Before they do, the reward center becomes highly active, leading the adolescent to pursue thrill-seeking behavior, but without an awareness of the consequences. Adults tend to have gut feelings (somatic imprinting from previous experiences) about the potential danger of a situation; adolescents, on the other hand, focus on potential positive outcomes, and it takes them a long time to weigh up the pros and cons before coming to a conclusion. For example, adults would instantly dismiss an idea such as "swimming with sharks" as dangerous. Adolescents might think, yes dangerous, but hmm . . . maybe also interesting, or cool, or fun?

Young people are able to understand risk in an environment that doesn't trigger their emotions, but as soon as their reward center is stimulated, they no longer see the potential consequences of their actions. An example she gives is an adolescent spending the money their mom has given them for a winter coat on a tattoo.

The part of the brain responsible for risk and daring is overactive in teenagers, and encourages them to try all kinds of sporting feats, like tricky stunts on a surf- or skateboard. Mirror neurons (special nerve cells) enable kids to learn simply by watching others do things – for example, a complicated sequence of dance steps.[7] Adults lose this ability. Musical talent also usually comes to the fore at this age (child prodigies like Mozart are extremely rare, Crone points out). Creativity and flexible thinking are positive attributes of the adolescent brain, as is mathematical ability. Adolescents have a great capacity to think outside the box.

In experiments modeling probable behavior patterns in a casino, adolescents usually opt for a small chance of winning a big profit over a large chance of winning a small profit. They are happier than adults with their winnings, and less upset by losses.[8] Research has also shown that adolescents make better decisions when a situation is explained as simply as possible. Crone interprets this in the following way: "It doesn't make much sense to explain all the possible risks of any specific choices an adolescent makes. Instead, it's more sensible to tell them that certain choices simply aren't good."[9]

Tests conducted at Leiden University show that "although young people showed less brain activity than adults after receiving negative feedback, it turned out that they showed more brain activity when receiving positive feedback. Apparently, young people's brains are more focused on getting encouragement and affirmation but gain less from punishment and censure."[10] Here we can see again the benefits of positive encouragement. Dutch parents practice this regularly, dropping positive comments casually into their daily conversations with their kids.

One final thing: Teenage kids may drive you mad by sleeping all morning and staying up all night, but many teenagers find it hard to get to sleep in the evenings because of the delayed release of melatonin in the adolescent brain. However, they need lots of sleep in order to grow. This can cause a chronic sleep deficit, which exacerbates behavioral problems. Crone recommends letting teenagers sleep in on the weekends and during vacation. They are not being lazy; they simply need all that extra sleep to develop and grow. There are moves in the Netherlands to start the secondary school day later, in acknowledgment of the fact that teenagers need more sleep and their brains function better later in the day.

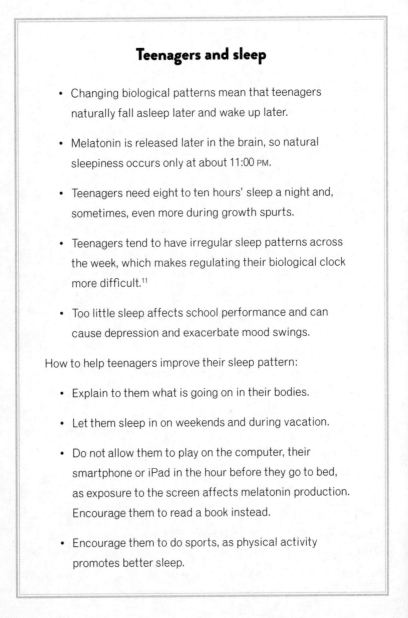

Teenagers and sleep

- Changing biological patterns mean that teenagers naturally fall asleep later and wake up later.

- Melatonin is released later in the brain, so natural sleepiness occurs only at about 11:00 PM.

- Teenagers need eight to ten hours' sleep a night and, sometimes, even more during growth spurts.

- Teenagers tend to have irregular sleep patterns across the week, which makes regulating their biological clock more difficult.[11]

- Too little sleep affects school performance and can cause depression and exacerbate mood swings.

How to help teenagers improve their sleep pattern:

- Explain to them what is going on in their bodies.

- Let them sleep in on weekends and during vacation.

- Do not allow them to play on the computer, their smartphone or iPad in the hour before they go to bed, as exposure to the screen affects melatonin production. Encourage them to read a book instead.

- Encourage them to do sports, as physical activity promotes better sleep.

I get talking to a former colleague back home, and she mentions the problems she is having with her teenage stepchildren. She calls the current debacle "a social media meltdown." Her fourteen-year-old stepdaughter has made all kinds of dubious friends online, including dope smokers and someone currently under house arrest. I ask whether the school is aware of this problem among its students, and she says that, although there have been talks and films on the subject at school, it hasn't helped. The children know the dangers but don't believe anything will happen to *them*. One classmate is trying to arrange to meet up with an older man, who has promised to buy her expensive shoes. "She doesn't see the danger," says my friend. "She thinks she can handle it."

I'm sure this all happens in Holland as well, but I wonder if teenagers here are more independent and more confident and so less vulnerable? I ask various Dutch parents whether they monitor their children's use of the internet and how susceptible to danger they think they are. Most of the parents I talk to don't think their children are particularly at risk; they trust them to be sensible about the friends they make online, and they follow certain rules, like never giving out an address or phone number. Annemarie, the mother of one of Ben's friends, has four children, including a teenage daughter. "I'm not very protective by nature," she tells me when I ask about her relationship with her thirteen-year-old. "And she's very streetwise, which means I can trust her. Sometimes, I casually bring up stuff, like people posting naked selfies on social media, and she gives me a look like *Do you think I'm crazy?*" Annemarie goes on to make another interesting point: "Sometimes I get the idea that people who have fewer children are more overprotective. I've got four children and a job, so I have to be driven by what's practical."

My sister-in-law Sabine says she was never worried about her daughter. She explained to her children why there were certain rules: always letting her know where they were and what time they were coming home, coming home at the agreed time, not spending hours playing computer games, and so on. In terms of hard drugs, there was plenty of information available at school and it was also sometimes a topic of conversation at home. Another friend of mine, who lives in Rotterdam, tells me her thirteen-year-old daughter gave a talk about drugs at school. The subject is quite a popular choice for the *spreekbeurten* Dutch children are regularly expected to give; there are even web pages tailored toward this topic.

Now, Sabine's eldest two children say that they see the value of her rules. "Sometimes, I get the idea you have to protect them from themselves," she says. "It must have been much simpler before, when there wasn't any daytime TV, the internet hadn't been invented and we didn't have mobile telephones." Like any other parent, she has tried to limit screen time and encourages her children to play outside instead. Half of her back garden is taken up by a dug-in trampoline and, even today, my nephews still like to bounce around on it.

Independence

I go to talk to one of my neighbors, Tessa, the elder sister of my friend Arwen, who makes children's films. She has two daughters aged fifteen and seventeen who are in the academic stream at a popular central Amsterdam school. They live in a beautiful dike house with blue peeling clapboard. Tessa counts herself lucky that both her daughters are reasonable and responsible. She says she has very few problems with them; it seems that sensible early parenting has paid off. The proverbial leash has been slowly lengthened. For her, the challenge now is "to find a balance" and work out the extent to which she needs to "guide, limit or restrict and let go" of her teenagers. "Letting go means accepting that, sometimes, things can go wrong," she adds.

By now, her daughters are already quite independent. She says you shouldn't try to give teenagers too much unsolicited advice but help them to make up their own minds. Hers haven't had any problems with gaming or social media, so I ask about her approach to alcohol and drugs. (The legal age for alcohol and cannabis consumption is eighteen, and "coffee shops," which sell cannabis, have a strict ID policy.) "It's best not to forbid anything," she says. "They don't drink spirits, but I know they've had wine and beer on occasion. I don't think that smoking pot is that bad, and I know they've tried it. Some of these things are important within a particular friendship group. They want to fit in. More important is to make them aware of their choices. They need to learn to recognize their own limits. After that, you can trust them. And up to now, nothing has ever gone wrong."

I like this liberal approach and can see why it appeals to the teenagers themselves. Like Sabine, Tessa and her husband negotiate the rules or, rather, make specific arrangements – for example, what time they are going to return – each time the girls go out or do some kind of activity outside the home. The family makes a point of eating breakfast and dinner together each day, giving ample opportunity for these discussions to take place. The concept of sitting down around a table to talk is crucial to this Dutch family, as it is to many others.

As mentioned above, she limits screen time to after 5:30 PM. And she doesn't monitor her daughters' homework; they have to do it by themselves. I can see how important this is. An expat father I know has helped with his daughter's homework from day one. Now, at eighteen and in her final year of school, she is unable to study on her own and demands his constant help and support. I, personally, would not want to get into this situation, and I wonder how she'll cope at university. If a parent always supervises their child's homework, it's easy to get into a situation where it isn't done without a lot of nagging and pleading from the parent, and the teenager will never start taking responsibility for it.

I ask Tessa if she has any regrets. "If there was one thing I wished I'd done differently, it would be to get them to help around the house at an earlier age, so that they would do so spontaneously by now. But you can't do everything right!"

Fear of failure

Wherever you live, adolescence is a time for children to experiment and discover who they are. Dutch parents seem to factor this in, in a calm, sensible manner. They tend not to get into conflict with their older kids but, instead, offer them support. Though a teenager may appear overconfident, perhaps brash and difficult, this is often really just a front for fear and insecurity.

The concept of *faalangst* – a handy Dutch word meaning "fear of failure" – is big in the Netherlands. While I have little sense of children being driven hard to perform here, attention is paid to things that might hold a child back, from dyslexia or ADHD to simple performance anxiety (despite the lack of competition). At primary schools, there isn't really much of an opportunity to experience failure, but at secondary school it's certainly possible to fail exams and have to repeat a year as a result, or to be moved into a lower stream and away from your friends. But help is at hand. Many schools have training programs to help children suffering from *faalangst*. It would certainly have helped me as a child.

I'm not aware of there being any particular evidence of British schools taking fear of failure seriously, though my mother, who is a special-needs advisor, mentions that it is just starting to come onto her radar. "There is more awareness of the problems due to high-profile suicides of bright pupils," she says. "People are just starting to look at the development of resilience and how that can be improved." I get her to raise the subject matter of stress management in schools with the headmaster of her local one and he asks around. This reply comes back: "No, secondary schools in England (well, the ones I contacted) don't run any stress-management lessons or courses. But [when I brought it up] it got some of them thinking!"

Over here, on the other hand, Ben's new school advertises on its website a staff member who offers fear-of-failure coaching, as do many other schools. The son of one of my book club members was identified as someone who would benefit from confidence-boosting training in his first term of secondary school, and it has helped him enormously.

Here in the Netherlands, there is plenty of more general help at hand for the parents, too; the trusty puberty guide, for example, mentions "parenting courses and drop-in clinics all over the country."

Fear of failure: advice to give your teens[12]

1. Work out exactly what it is you are afraid of. What are the particular situations that make you fearful? How do you act and think? Making the problem concrete makes it easier to tackle.
2. Prepare thoroughly for situations that make you anxious (e.g., exams).
3. Learn to interrupt any negative chains of thought, and to stop brooding and fretting.
4. Learn to tackle the physical signs of stress through relaxation, meditation, deep breathing, and so on.
5. Take a break when the pressure gets too much. During an exam, go to the restroom or have a sip of water.
6. Set realistic, achievable goals for yourself. Don't set the bar too high.
7. Take credit for success when credit is due. Don't put all your successes and failures down to chance.
8. Give yourself permission to make mistakes, and learn from them.
9. If you have an off day, don't let it affect your overall sense of self-worth.
10. Visualize success, not failure.

Popular Dutch parenting courses, typically held in community centers, libraries and schools, include "Getting on Better with Adolescents" and "Parenting Teenagers Positively." On the one hand, they counsel, adolescents need space and freedom, and parents have to learn to take a step back in their children's lives; on the other, adolescents – partly due to developmental patterns in their brain – need clear guidance. In addition to courses like these, there are also cabaret comedy acts that tour schools, illustrating the tensions between teenagers and parents in a lighthearted way.

A *gezellig* home full of teenagers

As luck would have it, a new parents' information evening is taking place at Ben's school. The topic is "Keeping Things *Gezellig* in the Home": how to maintain that cozy, social atmosphere the Dutch so love, even when you have sulky, hormonal teenagers. There will be a talk by a parenting expert who happens to also be an actress. I go along on my bike, braving the driving October rain. Ben's new school is located in a temporary building on the southwest bank of the river IJ. The colorful three-story block looks fun to me, nothing like the dreary trailers my own secondary school brought in whenever more space was needed. The dripping parents are invited into the hall, which is spacious and light. Next year, the new, improved school building will be ready, with the same characteristic red, yellow and orange stripes and wooden cladding.

Catharina Haverkamp welcomes the parents with something approaching a stand-up-comedy routine. A tall, gangly woman in her fifties, she has four children herself, between the ages of eleven and eighteen. She says it was parenting incompetence that led her to become an expert, the subtext being, "I'm no better than you." Her talk is going to be about *bemoediging* – which means both to comfort and to encourage. She claims it is the key to a happy home and good parenting.

She starts with a survey of the audience: how many children we have, how old they are, whether we worry about certain issues with regard to them, and so on. Stand up for yes; stay sitting for no. (This is a typically Dutch quiz technique; in the past, you would keep your cap on or take it off: *petje op, petje af*). I'm struck by the age of a lot of the parents here. The Dutch, in general, have their children later than anywhere else in the world. In addition, a high proportion of the audience has three or four children: Bigger families are typical of the Dutch middle class, as they have the resources, in terms of both time and money.

It becomes clear from Catharina's talk that, although unspoken, happiness is clearly the goal the parents share for their children. In a school in the US or the UK, I imagine the focus would be on grades and results. Like Lydwin, Catharina quotes adolescent-brain expert Eveline Crone, whose research has proved that a feeling of belonging is crucial to creating happiness in adolescents.

Nagging, she says, is a sign that a parent is afraid of their child failing, and fear offers poor counsel. She used to welcome her son home with that perennial parental favorite, "How was school?" and he'd scowl and remain taciturn, as most kids do. To the child, your concern can come across as you checking up on him, and puts a burden on him. It's better to trust your kids and show you have faith in them. "Don't lose sight of love," she advises. "A warm smile and no questions asked produces a better result." To be honest, I haven't yet had this problem with Ben; he's an unstoppable chatterbox and has always told me about his days in great detail, but I resolve to give the technique a try with Ina.

The core of Catharina's talk comes down to this: Don't be discouraging; be warmly encouraging and set a good example. Also, accept your child for the individual they are. Don't expect them to be like you, or who you wish you were. She produces a potted ficus and uses it as an example. The parents are asked to imagine that this is their child, but that really they wanted, say, a violet. The point is not to treat your ficus as though it were a violet. You don't ask it where the flowers are. You care for it according to what kind of plant it is. You look after the soil, add fertilizer; you don't start pulling off the leaves and trying to make it look like a different plant. The audience laughs.

When I chat with other parents at the end of the talk, they say they feel inspired by what they have heard. We talk about how our kids are coping with homework, in general, as it is new to them at secondary school, but there are no anxious comparisons. As I've mentioned several times, this is a social no-no.

Alcohol and drugs

As we've seen, Dutch teenagers have among the lowest rates of pregnancy and sexually transmitted diseases.[13] In addition, binge drinking, which is such a problem among teenagers in the UK, is not a behavior that Dutch parents of teenagers worry about. In an OECD study, the United Kingdom, Estonia and Denmark are at the top of the list, with the Netherlands last of the twenty-six countries surveyed, along with the US (because of stricter laws prohibiting underage drinking), Italy and Iceland. Research also suggests that children who have a good relationship with their parents drink less.[14] The number of Dutch children drinking and smoking is falling dramatically. Drug use here is an interesting issue because of the government's liberal approach. Although there are lots of "coffee shops" that sell marijuana, not only are they off-limits to under-eighteens, no coffee shop can operate within 250 meters (about one tenth of a mile) of a school. Official figures from 2011 state that around 19 percent of boys and 14 percent of girls of secondary school age have tried cannabis.[15] But if you ask the children themselves, they estimate that at least 80 percent smoke dope! My husband believes that the relative ease with which children can try cannabis makes the experience less of a thrilling prospect. He tried it himself as a teenager and thought, "So what?" It never became a habit.

Why Dutch teens are happy

When we met him back in the summer, Professor Ruut Veenhoven of Rotterdam's Erasmus University, aka the Happiness Professor, told us that his latest research had shown that Dutch adolescents were still the happiest in the world. "Most adolescents are happy, in fact," he said, "the Dutch just slightly more so." In the most recent World Health Organization study, 90 percent of Dutch girls and 96 percent of Dutch boys aged fifteen claimed "high life satisfaction." England and the US came eighteenth and twenty-second, respectively, but even there, around 80 percent of the fifteen-year-olds surveyed claimed they were happy.

We discussed why the Dutch had the edge on happiness in adolescents, and he put it down to there being a higher degree of "independence training" in the Netherlands. Kids have more freedom and are less overprotected than in other countries. He also mentioned his comparison of teaching practices in secondary schools, in which France stood out with its vertical method (teacher tells, student reproduces), whereas horizontal teaching (teacher acts as coach) prevails in Dutch schools. Vertical teaching undermines self-respect and autonomy, as does stiff competition.

The professor also pointed out the importance of there being readily available psychological help in Dutch schools, and that the relative economic equality in the country also helps. In the Netherlands, it is easier to feel content with what you have and there is less envy of other people's lifestyle. He adds, "I also think Dutch parents are less selective of their children's friends."

Friendships

One of the key factors in childhood happiness is your relationship with your peers and, in the 2013 UNICEF report, the Dutch won out again, with classmates found to be kind and helpful. The highest-scoring countries in terms of "finding classmates kind and helpful" were the Netherlands and Sweden.

A recent article in the *Guardian* claimed that English children were being made unhappy by the prevalence of bullying in schools.

> Violence and poor relationships with teachers puts English children fourteenth out of fifteen countries surveyed for happiness at school. Children in England are unhappier at school than their peers in almost every other country included in a new international survey, with widespread bullying causing huge damage to their wellbeing. An estimated half a million ten- and twelve-year-olds are physically bullied at school, according to a study by the Children's Society, which found that 38 percent of children surveyed had been hit by classmates in the last month.[16]

Margreet de Looze, an assistant professor at Utrecht University, responsible for the research behind the latest UNICEF report, told us that Dutch schools have very low ratings for bullying compared to other western countries, "even though parents might not realize this because there's such a lot of attention paid to bullying in the local media." (Dutch parents tend to be very vocal if there is something they are unhappy about.) "Wouldn't the absence of pressure and stress at school reduce bullying and make it easier to get on with your classmates?" I asked.

She agreed with my assessment of the situation. "And the lack of competition," she added. 'The Dutch score very low for feeling the pressure of schoolwork. Pressure is one of the most important determinants of happiness. I agree that it must affect the relationship between pupils."

When we asked her about the objectivity of the HBSC study she worked on, upon which UNICEF based its findings, Margreet told us, "Well, that is the question. Perhaps children rating themselves happy is a question of culture. We recognize that. But we do also look at objective well-being, not just subjective. For example, one part of the study examined health issues – headaches, stomachaches, sickness – these also can be used as indicators. The Dutch scored low here, too, so we do genuinely believe they are happier."

Conclusion: Let's Start a Revolution

Michele

As we are putting the finishing touches to this book, April comes round again. A year on, I'm back in the allotment, trying to get it into shape. The long, wet winter has turned the grass into an expanse of bumpy marshland, the kind that would give even a cow trench foot. The vegetable patch is filled with weeds and looks decidedly boggy, too. The children's raised boxes look fine: That's the way to go. Martijn is using the roller on the grass, trying to flatten it enough to be mowed. Ben has dug away a strip near the front fence so he can plant his wildflower meadow and butterfly garden, a project we attempt yearly and which has failed so far because the ground is too fertile and too wet. It prefers to produce stinging nettles and bindweed. I am attempting to pollard my young willow tree, randomly cutting back the branches to the crown and hoping it will in the end somehow resemble the ones that dot the Dutch countryside. The birds are singing and the daffodils are waving in the wind.

Now, the children are nine and eleven; the biggest changes in them are to do with increased independence. I doubt Ina will be stripping naked and playing in the wading pool this summer. She cycles to and from school on her own and sometimes hangs out at that ugly plastic-clad shopping center with her new girlfriends, trying on outfits in H&M. Luckily, she reads a lot, still plays football and is doing well at school. By coincidence, she's in the park with Tijn again today, playing outside with a group of friends, just like last year.

Ben is most of the way through his first year at secondary school and he manages to get up, make his packed lunch and arrive at school on time, with his homework completed and in his knapsack. I've been amazed by how high the academic level is at his *gymnasium*: For example, the Latin classes seem to have gone from zero to a hundred in sixty seconds. When Ben's not at school, he's at ballet and dance classes, but he has become addicted to watching vlogs on his phone. (I was warned.) His grades are pretty good, though not as good as those of his friend Floris, who is determined to join the academic stream next year. The vestiges of the ambitious Brit inside me are cheering him on.

There's no denying that being a parent in the Netherlands has changed the way Rina and I are bringing up our children. It has had an effect on our attitudes and how we think and feel about parenting. It has also altered how we behave.

Rina

For me, it has meant adopting a more relaxed approach to early schooling. Instead of worrying about little Julius' academic skills, I want to give him the time to develop through play. When Julius turns four shortly, we won't have a birthday party at home; he doesn't want one. Rather, we are going to take in mini-cupcakes and a rainbow cake on Julius' last day of preschool. He'll give away pencils with his picture on them to his classmates, with a note saying, "Thank you for playing with me. Love, Julius." And in the Dutch spirit of mini-getaways, our family will celebrate his birthday with a three-day visit to Efteling – a magical fairy tale theme park, established long before Disneyland. And there will be no Baby Einstein for baby Matteo either; instead, there will be rest and regularity. I have also stopped trying to prove myself the perfect mother by following my natural urge to seek out "the best" in everything for my children.

Michele

As for me, going Dutch has meant addressing my attitude to work and living a more balanced life. It has given me valuable weekend time to spend with my children, often outdoors at the allotment, or rollerblading around the park opposite our house. I am also starting to reap the benefits of learning to let go of my children so that they learn to be independent and solve problems on their own. Ben recently started Saturday classes at a professional dance academy on the other side of town, and the deal was that he'd get himself there on his own. The first time he was due to take public transport home, there was a demonstration in the center of Amsterdam. No trams were running. He telephoned me as he calmly made his way to the bus station on foot, past all the demonstrators – a distance of almost two miles (three kilometers). He was completely unfazed and managed to find his way without knowing that part of the city well. This must be the point of trusting one's child to be independent: developing in them resilience, problem-solving skills and unflappability.

———

We can't help but agree wholeheartedly with the UNICEF report: We believe it is true that the Dutch are raising the happiest kids in the world. Yet they aren't really doing anything new. They are doing things modern-day American and British parents were brought up on themselves but seem to have lost sight of in their concerted, overly ambitious drive to perfection. As far back as 1873, Birmingham obstetrician Pye Henry Chavasse advocated "fresh air, plain food and exercise" in his parenting guide *Advice to Mothers* and, in the eighteenth century, Jeremy Bentham, the founder of utilitarianism, thought that we should aim to make as many people happy as we can. Happiness should be central to life. "Seek to do good, rather than do well," he advised. Life should be about helping other people and taking good care of yourself and your children, not about comparing yourself to others. Spock's 1946 *Baby and Child Care* manual also appealed to common sense, opening with "Trust yourself. You know more than you think you do." The thing is, anyone can adopt the Dutch common-sense approach: It has been there all along, although it has recently been forgotten.

International OECD surveys show the importance of happiness in childhood: It is a strong indicator of welfare and success later in life. This is why the British Office of National Statistics ran its "Measuring National Well-being Programme" in 2012 and 2014 – it has become standard government policy to try to improve happiness.

What contributes to true happiness in a child?

- For babies and young children, the gift of a predictable routine: let them sleep, let them eat, keep them clean

- A home that is *gezellig*; a safe haven

- Parents who are there for them, and offer them unconditional love

- Being given the tools with which to gradually learn independence and self-reliance

- Having plenty of time to play

- Being given enough rules and boundaries to feel safe

"A lot of parents will do anything for their kids, except let them be themselves," British street artist Banksy writes, summing up a problem a lot of modern parents struggle with. The Dutch believe in learning for its own sake and in order to broaden the mind, not just to pass exams. Parents can help by not putting their children under pressure to perform. Forget academic hothousing. Put down the Baby Einstein and just go for a walk with your newborn. Let go of what you want your children to be and let them be themselves – imperfect, as we all are, but happy. Let kids be kids. Let them play.

Play can teach children so much. Active outdoor play is essential for growing kids, to train and develop their senses. Important senses are honed through rough and tumble. Encourage your child to go out and play in bad weather, so that they develop grit. And let them out, let them cycle and give them independence in controlled, incremental amounts.

Happiness is all about being friendly, rather than competitive, with your peers at school. The state itself should take steps to encourage this by continuing to rethink and reinvent the education system and narrow the gap of opportunity between rich and poor. It's no coincidence that politicians in the UK are currently lobbying for an education that promotes character, resilience and communication skills, rather than pushing children through exam factories. The Dutch are not educational pioneers: They are merely early adopters of proven, yet innovative, educational methods from other countries like Italy, Finland and Germany. They examine their own system of education and look elsewhere for new ideas that may improve it.

Happiness in children is allowing them the time and freedom for hobbies, without feeling that anything less than a gold medal counts as failure. Children with talent and passion are likely to become achievers anyway. And even then, let me be Dutch about this and put that into perspective for you – being a high achiever always comes at a cost. Is it really necessary?

Perhaps it is the human condition for each of us always to have a certain amount of anxiety that we have to make something of ourselves. If you live in a country where there are no acute problems, such as access to education, healthcare and affordable food and housing, perhaps it's natural to invent new problems. American parents often fall into the trap of wanting to give their kids everything they didn't have – whether it's unlimited Lego, unlimited parental attention or getting them into the "best" school. But this drive to do something positive for your child could be better channeled into teaching them to become independent and self-sufficient by gradually lengthening the leash. To quote the Happiness Professor Ruut Veenhoven, "If they don't fall, they don't learn."

You only have one childhood, and it lays the foundation for the rest of your life. Our knowledge of this can lead us to turn childhood into a problem. Parents are hyperaware of all the risks their babies are exposed to. We remember only too well cherishing those last months of our first pregnancies, when our babies were still safe in the womb. We were aware that pregnancy was the only time we would be fully in control of our children's whereabouts. But we parents need to mediate our constant fear that something bad will happen to our children. We need to put things into perspective for their sake. If we don't, the real world will come as a nasty shock to them.

Is there a cure for hyper-parenting? Well, for a start, the more children you have, the less time you have to hover over them. Time and energy have to be shared around; unlike love, it is limited. Parents with more than one child often look back and laugh at their anxious behavior with their firstborn. Helicopter parents often blame external factors – schools, teachers, other people – but they'd be better off addressing their own anxieties. Parents with feelings of inferiority have a tendency to try to live vicariously through their children's achievements, to compensate for their perceived failures. But that is selfish. What children need is love, encouragement, support and affection. Your child is a separate autonomous being, not an extension of their parents. One of the biggest lessons to learn as a parent is that your child is not a mini version of you.

In the Netherlands, parents are more likely to be self-fulfilled and independent and to enjoy their own lives. They are not overly protective, because they trust the society around them to cater to their needs and to those of their children. Independence and autonomy make people happy. So does dialogue. Having dinner together as a family and just talking to your children is a good start. If the buck stops here with the parents, the culture of overwork should stop here, too. It is up to employers to meet the needs of their employees, and up to employees to fight for them.

Happiness is a loving family and a good relationship with your parents – positive, supportive parents, not nagging, anxious ones. Parents' positive attitudes will improve their children's self-confidence. Their confidence will enable the kids to solve their own problems.

Parents in individualistic societies like the US and the UK tend to take on sole responsibility for their offspring. Perhaps it is time for a social revolution. This would require not just parents but society as a whole to step up to the challenge. Cultural changes are already happening, with greater flexibility in the workplace: There is an increase in the number of people working part-time, and as freelancers and portfolio workers combining different jobs. But the Dutch example shows that this could be taken much further. It makes sense to think about more cooperative childcare, for example: We're not rearing our children in a vacuum, and Dutch parents show us how to share responsibility with other parents, grandparents and neighbors, which takes the pressure off busy working parents. Research at the University of Leiden has shown that this kind of social safety net can contribute significantly to keeping children on the straight and narrow in later life.

We have learned such a lot about the character of the Dutch in our lives here as mothers. One of the things we have found most difficult to come to terms with is the value they put on averageness. The popular saying "Just act normal" sums it up. The Dutch like to put things into perspective, with humor and self-deprecation, and there is much less focus here on status and success. Though the country is not entirely classless (there is no such thing as a classless society), class does not define identity and shape lives the way it does in Britain, and neither does wealth define status the way it does in America. Here, even the royals ride bikes.

Herman Pleij writes that, for more than five centuries, the Netherlands has been one of the happiest societies in the world. He puts this down not to the number of millionaires, but to "the feeling that you are given your due here." In the interviews we have carried out or when we have discussed the ideas in this book with friends, Dutch people were frequently surprised to hear how positively we viewed their country, their parenting style and their culture. The tendency here is to look up to America as a cultural leader and to import its trends wholesale.

The Dutch National Social Policy Unit, which also runs research on well-being, found that 82 to 87 percent of the population would describe themselves as happy. The reasons given for this were decentralization, equality, personal initiative, individual commitment, self-reliance, pragmatism and a feeling of belonging. Individual life satisfaction recorded was, on average, 7.8 out of 10. And yet, in *"Sturen op geluk"* (Steering toward happiness), a research paper by Dutch sociologist Paul Schnabel, it says that, while at least four fifths of Dutch people say they are happy, only 1 percent of the population thinks that the country is heading in the right direction. The irony is that the Dutch themselves all think the Netherlands is going to the dogs!

In the English-speaking world, the obsession with getting ahead in the rat race has built-in consequences for society. There aren't millions of amazing jobs to be had anymore, there isn't an infinite amount of money to be made, so market forces drive a Darwinist attitude of the survival of the fittest. But does this view really make sense? Are the Dutch ultimately less successful as a whole by not pursuing the same path as others in the Western world? No. Isn't the goal of producing happy kids the best goal of all?

Notes

Introduction

1 The UNICEF report drew on research conducted by the World Health Organization; see hbsc.org.

2 Jimin Sung et al., "Exploring Temperamental Differences in Infants from the USA and the Netherlands," *European Journal of Developmental Psychology* 12, no. 1 (2015): 15–28.

3 T. Berg-le Clercq, *The Dutch Family in International Perspective* (Utrecht: Netherlands Youth Institute, 2009), nji.nl.

4 Organisation for Economic Co-operation and Development (OECD), "Average Annual Hours Actually Worked per Worker," stats.oecd.org/Index.aspx?DataSetCode=ANHRS.

5 The Dutch came fifth in Health and Safety in the 2013 UNICEF report, behind Scandinavian countries like Iceland, Sweden, Finland and Luxembourg.

Chapter One: Discovering Dutchland

1 In the Netherlands, statutory maternity leave is shorter than in the UK – a rare example among childcare matters where the country lags behind.

2 Katie Morley, "We Earn £190k a Year. Do We Need to Sell Our Flat to Afford Private School Fees?" *Telegraph*, November 19, 2015, telegraph.co.uk.

Chapter Two: Mothering the Mother

1 Raymond de Vries, *A Pleasing Birth* (Philadelphia: Temple University Press, 2004).

2 *The Urban Disadvantage: State of the World's Mothers 2015* (Fairfield, CT: Save the Children, 2015).

3 "Births – Method of Delivery," Centers for Disease Control and Prevention, last updated October 7, 2016, cdc.gov/nchs/fastats/delivery.htm.

4 Marian F. MacDorman, T. J. Matthews, and Eugene Declercq, "Trends in Out-of-Hospital Births in the United States 1990–2012," National Center for Health Statistics data brief, no. 144 (2014), cdc.gov/nchs/data/databriefs/db144.pdf.

5 Lindsay Beyerstein, "Why the Netherlands Is a Red Herring in the Home Birth Debate," *Slate*, July 6, 2012, slate.com.

6 Rachel Halliwell, "Conveyor-Belt Maternity Units: 'I Was Told to Go Home 6 Hours after Giving Birth,'" *Telegraph*, December 31, 2014, telegraph.co.uk.

Chapter Three: The Real Happiest Babies on the Block

1 Jan Abram, *The Language of Winnicott: A Dictionary of Winnicott's Use of Words*, 2nd ed. (London: Karnac, 2007).

2 Jennifer Kunst, "In Search of the 'Good-Enough Mother': How to Honor the Complexity of Motherhood," *Psychology Today*, May 9, 2012.

3 Jesse Singal, "Dutch Babies: Better than American Babies?" *New York* magazine, January 29, 2015, nymag.com.

4 Ian Johnston, "Global Sleeping Study Reveals Women Get More than Men," *Independent*, May 6, 2016, independent.co.uk.

5 Anneke Kesler, *Growth Guide: Ages 0–4*, Gemeentelijke Geneeskundige Dienst, groeigids.nl.

6 Jennifer Slatton, "Sleeping Like a Baby," *New Beginnings* 20, no. 1 (January–February 2003), llli.org/nb/nbjanfeb03p4.html.

7 Sara Harkness and Charles M. Super, eds., *Parents' Cultural Belief Systems: Their Origins, Expressions and Consequences* (New York: Guilford Press, 1996).

8 Sara Harkness et al., "Parental Ethnotheories of Children's Learning," in *The Anthropology of Learning in Childhood*, ed. David F. Lancy, John Bock, and Suzanne Gaskins, (Lanham, MD: AltaMira Press, 2010).

9 Ibid.

Chapter Four: Joyful Illiterate Preschoolers

1 Daphna Bassok, Scott Latham, and Anna Rorem, "Is Kindergarten the New First Grade?" *AERA Open* 2, no. 1 (January 6, 2016). Researchers compared American public school kindergarten classrooms between 1998 and 2010 using two nationally representative data sets and uncovered a dramatic shift in expectations of kindergartners. Teachers in the later period held kindergartners to a far higher academic standard, devoting more time to formal teacher-directed instruction on literacy and math.

Chapter Five: Stress-Free Schooling

1 "How to Make Your Kid Smarter," medium.com, June 3, 2015.

2 Heather Shumaker, "Homework Is Wrecking Our Kids: The Research Is Clear, Let's Ban Elementary Homework," *Salon*, March 5, 2016, salon .com.

Vicki Abeles, "We're Destroying Our Kids – for Nothing: Too Much Homework, Too Many Tests, Too Much Needless Pressure," *Salon*, October 31, 2015, salon.com.

Jordan Rosenfeld, "Homework Is Making Our Kids Miserable: Why the Classroom Staple Is a Colossal Waste of Time," *Salon*, March 13, 2015, salon.com.

Alfie Kohn, "Homework: An Unnecessary Evil? . . . Surprising Findings from New Research," *Washington Post*, November 26, 2012, washingtonpost.com.

3 Nicola Woolcock, "Students in Crisis over Poor Maths and English," *Times*, January 29, 2016.

4 "Britse tieners onder minst geletterden van westerse wereld," *Het Parool*, February 8, 2016.

5 Deep-fried sausages: a typical Dutch snack.

6 World Database of Happiness, worlddatabaseofhappiness.eur.nl.

7 Inspectie van het Onderwijs, *De staat van den onderwijs: Onderwijsverslag 2013/2014* (Utrecht: Inspectie van het Onderwijs, 2015), onderwijsinspectie.nl/documenten/publicaties/2015/04/15/de-staat-van-het-onderwijs-onderwijsverslag-2013-2014.

8 Herman Pleij, *Moet kunnen: Op zoek naar een Nederlandse identiteit* (Amsterdam: Prometheus, 2014), 162.

9 Ibid, xxii.

10 Peter Gray, "The Decline of Play and Rise in Children's Mental Disorders," *Psychology Today*, January 26, 2010.

11 OECD, *How's Life? 2015: Measuring Well-Being* (Paris: OECD Publishing, 2015).

12 I was very surprised to see Spain and Turkey taking the lead. Then again, I know little about their school systems.

13 Bruno Waterfield, "OECD Education Report: Dutch System Puts Premium on Quality Standards," *Daily Telegraph*, December 3, 2013, telegraph.co.uk.

14 Hanna Rosin, "The Silicon Valley Suicides: Why Are So Many Kids with Bright Prospects Killing Themselves in Palo Alto?" *Atlantic*, December 2015, theatlantic.com.

Chapter Six: On Discipline

1 Hiske Versprille, "Zijn kinderen straks niet meer welkom in de horeca?" *Het Parool*, August 21, 2015.

2 "Straffen" (Punishment), Onderwijsgeschiedenis (Education history), onderwijsgeschiedenis.nl/Straffen.

3 Fanta Voogd, "Laat de kinderen vrij spelen," *Ons Amsterdam*, onsamsterdam.nl.

4 Triple P Positive Parenting Program website, triplep-parenting.com/us-en/triple-p.

5   Sheila Sitalsing, "Ik ga je rammelen," *de Volkskrant*, May 30, 2015, volkskrant.nl/leven/ik-ga-je-rammelen~a4041019.

6   Kok, Rianne, "'Do as I Say!' Parenting and the Biology of Child Self-Regulation," doctoral dissertation, Leiden University, 2013.

7   Fiona Macrae, "Toddlers Have a Strong Sense of Justice: Biscuit-Stealing Experiment Shows Infants Inherently Know Right from Wrong," *Daily Mail*, June 18, 2015, dailymail.co.uk.

Chapter Seven: Biking through the Rain

1   "Dutch people who cycle regularly live on average half a year longer than those who don't." "Lang leve de fietser" (Long live the biker), Utrecht University News, June 22, 2015, uu.nl/nieuws/lang-leve-de-fietser.

2   fietsersbond.nl. The Dutch Union of Cyclists' website provides a range of information (in Dutch).

3   Fanfare "Bereden Wapens" (FBW); the orchestra consists of twenty-two musicians on bicycles.

4   According to the UK Road Traffic Act, two people are not allowed to ride on a single bike unless the cycle is "constructed or adapted for the carriage of more than one person" – i.e., a tandem or a bike with approved equipment such as a child seat. If you do carry a passenger on a bicycle not constructed or adapted for the purpose, you are breaking s.24 of the Road Traffic Act.

5   Joaquín T. Limonero et al., "Estrategias de afrontamiento resilientes y regulación emocional: Predictores de satisfacción con la vida" (Resilient coping strategies and emotional regulation: Predictors of life satisfaction), *Behavioral Psychology/Psicología Conductual* 20, no. 1 (January 2012): 183–96.

6   Marijke Bisschop, *Opvoeden in een verwenmaatschappij: Hoe maak ik mijn kind toch gelukkig?* (Tielt: Lannoo, 2005), 78.

7   "Fietshelmen" (Bicycle helmets), fietsersbond.nl/de-feiten/verkeer-en-veiligheid/fietshelmen.

8 SWOV (Institute for Road Safety Research), "Road Deaths in the Netherlands," SWOV fact sheet, June 2016, swov.nl/en/facts-figures/factsheet/road-deaths-netherlands.

9 Pete Jordan, *De fietsrepubliek: Een geschiedenis van fietsend Amsterdam* (Amsterdam: Podium, 2013).

10 "How Many People Cycle and How Often?" Cycling UK, last updated October 2016, ctc.org.uk/resources/ctc-cycling-statistics#How many people cycle and how often?

11 The name of the bike make Batavus, incidentally, refers to a mythical, ideal state inhabited by the Batavia tribe. These were the forefathers of the modern Dutch, according to sixteenth-century physician and classical scholar Hadrianus Junius, who wrote the first known book on Dutch identity.

Chapter Eight: A Childhood of Freedom

1 Johan de Bruijn and Ineke Strouken, *Typisch Nederland: Tradities en trends in Nederland* (Amsterdam: Reader's Digest, 2011), 51.

2 Gitty Feddema and Aletta Wagenaar, *En als we nou weer eens gewoon gingen opvoeden* (Houten: Spectrum, 2013), 162 (author's translation).

3 Annemiek Leclaire, "Het stadskind drinkt pumpkin latte," nrc.nl, November 7, 2015.

4 Amendment on p. 857 of the Every Student Succeeds Act. See Aarian Marshall, "The Legal Standing of Free-Range Parenting," *Atlantic*, January 11, 2016, theatlantic.com.

5 "Damiaan Denys," *Zomergasten* (a Dutch television in-depth interview program), August 30, 2015.

6 Christina Hardyment, *Dream Babies: Childcare Advice from John Locke to Gina Ford* (London: Frances Lincoln, 2007), 343.

7 Ibid, 347.

8 Diana Baumrind, "Effects of Authoritative Parental Control on Child Behavior," *Child Development* 37, no. 4 (December 1966): 887–907.

9 "Play's the Thing," University of Cambridge Research, August 4, 2015, cam.ac.uk/research/features/plays-thing.

Chapter Nine: The Simple Life

1 Information taken from Ineke Strouken, *Dit zijn wij: De 100 belangrijkste tradities van Nederland* (Beilen: Pharos, 2010), Chapter 51.

2 "Zakgeld: Hoeveel geef je?" (Pocket money: How much would you give?), NIBUD (National Institute for Family Finance Information), nibud.nl/consumenten/zakgeld.

3 Pleij, *Moet kunnen*, 14.

4 4 Ibid., 76

5 5 Richard Wilkinson and Kate Pickett, *The Spirit Level: Why Equality Is Better for Everyone*, (London: Penguin, 2010), 6.

6 6 Ibid., 7.

Chapter Ten: Happy Parents Have Happy Kids

1 Caroline Brothers, "Why Dutch Women Don't Get Depressed," *The New York Times*, June 6, 2007, nytimes.com.

2 Elissa Strauss, "Surprise, Surprise: American Parents Are the Least Happy Parents in the Western World," *Slate*, June 16, 2016, slate.com.

3 Jennifer Glass, "CCF Brief: Parenting and Happiness in 22 Countries," June 15, 2016, Council on Contemporary Families, contemporaryfamilies.org/brief-parenting-happiness.

4 "Employment Statistics," Eurostat Statistics Explained, ec.europa .eu/eurostat/statistics-explained/index.php/Employment_statistics. Taken from the table "Persons working part-time or with a second job, 2004–14" and the figure "Persons employed part-time, age group 20–64, 2014."

5 There is also parental leave – twenty-six times the number of hours you work per week, to be taken by the time your child turns eight.

6 Els Kloek, *Vrouw des huizes: Een cultuurgeschiedenis van de Hollandse huisvrouw* (Amsterdam: Balans, 2009), 7.

7 Ibid., 10.

8 Brigid Schulte, *Overwhelmed: How to Work, Love, and Play When No One Has the Time*, (London: Bloomsbury, 2014), 29.

9 "Vrouwen ervaren vrije tijd als minder ontspannend dan mannen," *Het Parool*, March 8, 2016, parool.nl.

10 If we compare the Dutch to the Americans, general stress for working mothers Stateside is much, much worse, to the degree that it could be affecting their children's happiness. Schulte writes: "The World Health Organization found that Americans live in the richest country, but they are also the most anxious. The average high-school kid today experiences the same level of anxiety as the average psychiatric patient of the 1950s. And perhaps more disturbingly, scientists are finding that when children are exposed to stress – often stemming from the overwhelm of their parents – it can alter not only their neurological and hormonal systems but also their very DNA." Schulte, *Overwhelmed*, 57.

11 Colin White and Laurie Boucke, *The UnDutchables: An Observation of the Netherlands, Its Culture and Its Inhabitants* (Amsterdam: Nijgh & Van Ditmar, 2004), 154.

12 OECD.Stat, "Level of GDP Per Capita and Productivity," stats.oecd.org/Index.aspx?DataSetCode=PDB_LV.

13 There's a movement in contemporary Dutch philosophy that argues that time spent idling in a relaxed state of deep thought is extremely helpful to anyone who works in a job in which they primarily use their intellectual abilities. See Joke Hermsen's bestselling work, *Stil de tijd* (Stop the clocks) (Amsterdam: Arbeiderspers, 2013).

14 OECD Better Life Index, "Work-Life Balance," oecdbetterlifeindex.org/topics/work-life-balance.

Chapter Eleven: It's All about the *Hagelslag*

1 White and Boucke, *The UnDutchables*, 94.

2 Putnam, Robert D., *Our Kids: The American Dream in Crisis* (New York: Simon and Schuster, 2015).

Chapter Twelve: Let's Talk about Sex

1 Rutgers for Sexual and Reproductive Rights, "Spring Fever," rutgers .international/what-we-do/comprehensive-sexuality-education/spring-fever.

2 Fifty-seven, fifty-one, and forty-seven pregnancies per 1,000 teenagers respectively in the US, New Zealand, and England and Wales. "Teen Pregnancy Rates Declined in Many Countries between the Mid-1990s and 2011," Guttmacher Institute news release, January 23, 2015, guttmacher.org/media/nr/2015/01/23.

3 weekvandelentekriebels.nl.

4 Haye van der Heyden, *Het geheim van de gebroken ruit* (Amsterdam: Leopold, 2009).

5 Strouken, *Dit zijn wij*, 54.

6 A. Pawlowski, "Target Removing 'Gender-Based Signage' for Kids after Complaints from Parents," today.com, August 10, 2015.

7 Sarah Womack, "The Generation of 'Damaged' Girls," *Telegraph*, February 20, 2007, telegraph.co.uk.

8 According to the APA's task force chair Eileen Zurbriggen: "The consequences of the sexualization of girls in media today are very real and are likely to be a negative influence on girls' healthy development. . . . As a society, we need to replace all these sexualized images with ones showing girls in positive settings. . . . The goal should be to deliver messages to all adolescents – boys and girls – that lead to healthy sexual development": "Sexualization of Girls Is Linked to Common Mental Health Problems in Girls and Women – Eating Disorders, Low Self-Esteem, and Depression; An APA Task Force Reports," American Psychological Association press release, February 19, 2007, apa.org.

Chapter Thirteen: Dutch Teenagers Don't Rebel

1 As with crèches, after-school clubs are subsidized for parents who earn below a certain threshold. Means-testing determines how much of a rebate you receive.

2 Simon Kuper, "Why American Teens Should Go Dutch," *Financial Times*, January 13, 2012, ft.com.

3 "*Ik heb hier een stel pubers in huis die al dagenlang het begrip 'lamlendigheid' haarscherp in kaart brengen*" (author's translation).

4 Sunny Bergman, "Frisgewassen consumentisme," September 16, 2015, vpro.nl/lees/columns/sunny-bergman/opvoeden.html.

5 *Groeigids: Puberteit*, Gemeentelijke Geneeskundige Dienst, p. 53. See also their (Dutch) website, groeigids.nl

6 Ibid., 36

7 Eveline Crone, *Het puberende brein* (Amsterdam: Bert Bakker, 2008), 160.

8 Ibid., 112–13.

9 Ibid., 116.

10 Ibid., 68.

11 "Teens and Sleep," National Sleep Foundation, sleepfoundation.org/sleep-topics/teens-and-sleep.

12 Adapted from Leiden University's list: "Tien tips bij faalangst," studietips.leidenuniv.nl/faalangst.html.

13 Centraal Bureau voor de Statisteik, "Number of Teenage Mothers Unprecedentedly Low," October 15, 2013, cbs.nl/en-gb/news/2013/42/number-of-teenage-mothers-unprecedentedly-low.

Thomas Rogers, "Solving America's Teen Sex Problem," *Salon*, October 30, 2011, salon.com.

Amy T. Schalet, *Not under My Roof: Parents, Teens, and the Culture of Sex* (Chicago: University of Chicago Press, 2011).

14 *Groeigids Puberteit*, 101.

15 Ibid.

16 Sally Weale, "English Children among the Unhappiest in the World at School Due to Bullying," *Guardian*, August 18, 2015, theguardian.com.

Bibliography

Books published in English

Chua, Amy. *The Battle Hymn of the Tiger Mother*. New York: Penguin, 2011.

De Vries, Raymond. *A Pleasing Birth: Midwives and Maternity Care in the Netherlands*. Philadelphia: Temple University Press, 2004.

Druckerman, Pamela, *Bringing Up Bébé: One American Mother Discovers the Wisdom of French Parenting*. New York: Penguin, 2012.

Geske, Colleen, *Stuff Dutch People Like*. Amsterdam: Stuff Dutch People Like, 2013.

Hardyment, Christina. *Dream Babies: Childcare Advice from John Locke to Gina Ford*. Londong: Frances Lincoln, 2007.

Jordan, Pete. *In the City of Bikes: The Story of the Amsterdam Cyclist*. New York: Harper Perennial, 2013.

Martin, Wednesday. *Primates of Park Avenue: A Memoir*. New York: Simon and Schuster, 2015.

Putnam, Robert D. *Our Kids: The American Dream in Crisis*. New York: Simon and Schuster, 2015.

Schalet, Amy T. *Not under My Roof: Parents, Teens, and the Culture of Sex*. Chicago: University of Chicago Press, 2011.

Schulte, Brigid. *Overwhelmed: How to Work, Love and Play When No One Has the Time*. London: Bloomsbury, 2014.

Shorto, Russell. *Amsterdam: A History of the World's Most Liberal City*. New York: Vintage, 2014.

White, Colin, and Laurie Boucke. *The UnDutchables: An Observation of the Netherlands, Its Culture and Its Inhabitants*. Amsterdam: Nijgh & Van Ditmar, 2004.

Wilkinson, Richard, and Kate Pickett. *The Spirit Level: Why Equality Is Better for Everyone*. London: Penguin, 2010.

Other publications in English

Currie, Candace, et al., eds. *Social Determinants of Health and Well-Being among Young People: Health Behaviour in School-Aged Children (HBSC) Study: International Report from the 2009/2010 Survey*. Copenhagen: WHO Regional Office for Europe, 2012.

Organisation for Economic Co-operation and Development, *How's Life? 2015: Measuring Well-Being*. Paris: OECD Publishing, 2015.

Wouters, Cas. "'Not under My Roof': Teenage Sexuality and Status Competition in the USA and the Netherlands since the 1880s." *Human Figurations* 3, no. 2 (June 2014).

Books published in Dutch

Bisschop, Marijke. *Opvoeden in een verwenmaatschappij: Hoe maak je je kind toch gelukkig?* Tielt: Lanoo, 2005.

Botermans, Jack, and Wim van Grinsven. *Gezelligheid kent geen tijd: Nederland en zijn tradities, van kaatsen tot carnaval tot haringhappen*. Arnhem: Terra, 2010.

Crone, Eveline, *Het puberende brein*. Amsterdam: Bert Bakker, 2008.

de Bruijn, Johan, and Ineke Strouken. *Typisch Nederlands: Tradities en trends in Nederland*. Amsterdam: Reader's Digest, 2011.

Feddema, Gitty, and Aletta Wagenaar. *En als we nou weer eens gewoon gingen opvoeden*, rev. ed. Houton: Spectrum, 2013.

Kloek, Els. *Vrouw des huizes: Een cultuurgeschiedenis van de Hollandse huisvrouw*. Amsterdam: Balans, 2009.

Margreet de Looze et al. *HBSC 2013: Gezondheid, welzijn en opvoeding van jongeren in Nederland*. Utrecht: Universiteit Utrecht, 2014.

Pleij, Herman. *Moet kunnen: Op zoek naar een Nederlandse identiteit*. Amsterdam: Prometheus, 2014.

Strouken, Ineke. *Dit zijn wij: De 100 belangrijkste tradities van Nederland*. Beilen: Pharos, 2010.

van Erp, Barbara, and Femke Sterken. *Dit is het boek voor ouders met een leven*. Amsterdam: Nijgh & Van Ditmar, 2015.

Acknowledgments

Thanks to Marianne Velmans of Doubleday for coming up with the brilliant idea for this book, commissioning us to write it and then nursing it as if it were her very own baby. Thanks to Lizzy Goudsmit for her careful streamlining of the text, Kate Samano, and Sarah Day for her thorough copyediting.

Thanks to Batya Rosenblum for her sensitive, attentive editing of the text for the American edition and to all the cool folks at The Experiment.

Transworld: the Rights team: Helen Edwards, Ann-Katrin Ziser, Josh Crosley; Sophie Christopher from Publicity and Alice Murphy-Pyle from Marketing.

Thanks to Elik Lettinga for decisively snapping up the Dutch rights.

Thanks to our experts: Margreet de Looze, Professor Ruut Veenhoven, Roos Wouters, Els Kloek and Professors Sara Harkness and Charles Super.

Michele's support crew: Martijn, Ben and Ina, Arwen van Grafhorst, Paulien Mouwen, Thomas Durner and Heleen Suer, the lovely ladies of Noord Leest, Lesley Wolsey, Joanna Nakopoulou and Iain Wolsey, Eline and Mattijn van Ling, Roman Krznaric, the kids at Montessori School Boven 't IJ, Dineke Valenkamp, Cinthya van Bakel, Lydwin van Rooyen, Janneke Horn, Helen Garnons-Williams, Simon Prosser, Leyla Moghadam, Leilah Bruton, Kirsty Dunseath, Tessa van Grafhorst, Sabine David, Madea Le Noble, Victoria Silver, Francine Brody, Mel Rush, Arnold Auée, Gonda Bruijn, Katrien Hoekstra, Joris Luyendijk, Anne Marie Vaalburg.

Rina's team: Bram, Junior and Matteo, Hester Velmans, my parents Julio and Thelma Acosta, Rhada Rhamcharan, Elma Van Biljon, Eva Brouwer, Tara Wood, Abdelkader Benali, Doortje Graafmans, Mark Hoetjer, Mariska Schoutens, Esther Buitendijk, Ottilie Cools, Maria van Lieshout, Gowri Krishna, Anne Leenheer, Dingena Kortland, Irma Lauffer, Leilah Bruton, Marc Möderscheim, Jet van der Hoeven, Ewoud Verheij, Jop de Kwaadste-niet, Michelle Barrionuevo-Mazzini, Frans Liefhebber, Anton de Jong.

Index

About the Authors

Rina Mae Acosta is an Asian American writer from San Francisco currently living in the Netherlands with her Dutch husband and two young sons. She holds degrees from the University of California, Berkeley, and Erasmus University in Rotterdam. She is the author of a successful parenting blog, *Finding Dutchland*.

Michele Hutchison is an editor, translator and blogger. She was born in Solihull, England, grew up in Lincolnshire and studied at the universities of East Anglia, Cambridge and Lyon. She worked in British publishing before moving to Amsterdam, heavily pregnant, in 2004. There she worked as an editor and became a prominent translator of Dutch literature. She lives in a leaky old dike house with her Dutch husband and two children.